"Now that there is such good and wonderfully varied material to be had, it is all the more encouraging to make Rose gardens more beautiful, not with beds of Roses alone...but to consider the many different ways in which Roses not only consent to grow but in which they live most happily and look their best."

ROSES FOR ENGLISH GARDENS.

BY

GERTRUDE JEKYLL

AND

EDWARD MAWLEY.

ANTIQUE COLLECTORS' CLUB

© 1982 The Estate of Gertrude Jekyll
World copyright reserved
Reprinted 1987

ISBN 0 907462 24 3

First published by Country Life/George Newnes Ltd., 1902.
This edition, with 24 colour illustrations, published in 1982
for the Antique Collectors' Club by the Antique Collectors'
Club Ltd.

Reprinted 1990

British Library CIP Data
Jekyll, Gertrude
    Roses for English gardens
    1. Roses
    I. Title   II. Mawley, Edward
    635.9'33372   SB411

Printed in England by the Antique Collectors' Club Ltd., Woodbridge, Suffolk

CONTENTS

PART I

OLD AND NEW GARDEN ROSES AND THEIR BEAUTIFUL USE IN GARDENS

BY GERTRUDE JEKYLL

CONTENTS

PART II

PLANTING, PRUNING, AND PROPAGATING ROSES; EXHIBITING, GROWING UNDER GLASS, ETC.

By EDWARD MAWLEY

PREFACE

ONE of the surest signs of the great and ever-growing interest in gardening is to be seen in the remarkable improvement in the kinds of flowers that are now to be had. New plants are being constantly introduced; good old plants, of late forgotten, are again brought forward, and a lively and wholesome competitive industry has increased among growers in the improvement of garden flowers. In no class of plant is this more apparent than among the Roses. The increasing desire to deck our gardens pictorially has been met by a truly surprising and successful series of efforts on the part of raisers, so that now, in addition to the older classes of Roses that have been available for the last forty years, namely, the Hybrid Perpetuals and Teas, there are already, in great variety, quantities of beautiful new Roses of mixed parentage for every possible use and purpose.

The time having come when there is a distinct need for a book that shall not only show how Roses may best be grown, but how they may be most beautifully used, and that will also help the amateur to acquire some idea of their nature and relationships, the present volume, with its large amount of illustration, is offered in the hope that it will fit usefully into a space as yet unfilled in garden literature.

In order that the book may be a complete Rose manual, I have had the pleasure of working in concert with Mr. Edward Mawley, who, in the second part, gives the result of his long experience as a practical rosarian.

I have to offer grateful acknowledgment to Miss Willmott for a considerable number of excellent photographs, and for valuable help in compiling the list of Rose species as garden plants; to Mr. W. Robinson for permission to reproduce some Rose portraits from former coloured plates in *The Garden;* to Mr. Edward Woodall for the chapter on Riviera Garden Roses; to Mr. E. T. Cook for frequent advice and assistance, and to the owners of *The Garden* and *Country Life* for a number of the illustrations.

Lists of Roses for special purposes are given at the end of some of the chapters where it appeared that they would be most of use. At the end of the book are also descriptive lists, and an alphabetical list of the best Roses in all classes. A note of the abbreviations used against the Rose names appears on page 372. It will be understood that the lists of the Roses given are not complete lists of all the Roses known, but careful and well-proved selections of the best.

G. J.

PART I

OLD AND NEW GARDEN ROSES AND THEIR BEAUTIFUL USE IN GARDENS

By GERTRUDE JEKYLL

ROSES FOR ENGLISH GARDENS

CHAPTER I

GARDEN ROSES NEW AND OLD

NEW GARDEN ROSES

ONE of the most distinct and wholesome effects of
the spread of garden knowledge and love of flowers
that has filled the land of late years is the demand for
good garden Roses. By the term "garden Roses,"
is meant Roses for ordinary garden use, though the
word has a more exclusive use in the schedules of
Rose Societies, where it means any Roses other than
those that are classed as show kinds. In this case
the more rigid distinction is of use, though in the
garden it does not concern us in the least, for it
naturally happens that a grand show Rose is often
a grand garden Rose also.

But in the usual jargon of horticulture the word
"garden Rose" makes one first think of Damask
and Provence or Cabbage Roses, of Moss Roses,
of Sweet Brier and Scotch Brier, of Cinnamon Rose
and *Rosa lucida*, of China Rose, and of the old climbing cluster kinds; in short, of all the older favourites
that will grow readily in any garden in answer to
reasonable care and preparation.

13

It is only of late years, since an increased recognition of the delights of the garden has spread anew throughout Britain, and is rapidly extending through her colonies, that any notable additions have been made to the garden Roses. But our best Rose growers have not been slow to perceive how gladly their good new garden Roses have been welcomed ; the success of these has encouraged further effort, and whereas a few years ago lists of new Roses were mostly attractive to specialists, and consisted almost exclusively of Hybrid Perpetuals and Teas, the new Rose lists of to-day include kinds that appeal to every one who loves a garden.

The reason for the older limitation may be easily understood, for whereas success in growing the show Roses depends, to begin with, either on the possession of a good Rose soil, or on those qualifications of knowledge, determination, and command of money that can create one where it does not exist, the wants of the free and "garden" Roses are so comparatively modest, they are so accommodating and so little fastidious, that with very moderate preparation and encouragement they can be made to succeed in much poorer soils. Then it is but few that aspire to the honours of the show table, while nearly every one who is master of a rood of land now desires to enjoy it as a garden.

So it has come about that one after another, more and more garden Roses have come into use and have come into being. One of the first of the outsiders to be adopted as a garden Rose was the

CRIMSON RAMBLER (Cl. Poly.)

DOUBLE ROSA POLYANTHA (WHITE RAMBLER).

Himalayan *R. Brunoni* or *moschata*, with its rambling habit, its pale bluish leaves, and its clusters of milk-white bloom. Then we took up the type *Rosa multiflora* or *polyantha*, with its vigorous growth and its multitudes of Bramble-like sweet-scented flowers. Then Turner's Crimson Rambler, a plant of Japanese origin, closely related to *R. multiflora*, took the garden world by storm, for its easy cultivation, great speed of growth, and its masses of showy crimson bloom. Those of us whose eyes are trained to niceties of colour-discrimination wish that the tint of this fine flower had been just a shade different. Brilliant it undoubtedly is, and its noonday brightness gives pleasure to a great number of people; but if it had had just a little less of that rank quality that it possesses slightly in excess, it would have been a still more precious thing in our gardens. The time to see it in perfection is when the sun is nearing the horizon, and when the yellow light, neutralising the purplish taint, gives the flowers of the Rambler just the quality that they unfortunately lack; then and then only they show the glorious red that the critical colour-eye demands, while at the same time their brilliancy is intensified.

From the type *multiflora* and some of its hybrids as parents on one side have arisen a range of garden Roses of inestimable value, most of them of rambling habit, comprising the rose-coloured Dawson, the charming pink Euphrosyne, the white Thalia and the yellow Aglaia, followed by Leuchtstern, a charming pillar Rose with pink, red-tinted, white-eyed flowers, Waltham Rambler and Eleanor Berkeley, and Psyche, rosy-pink slightly tinted yellow. From the same source on one side there are also Lion and Wallflower, crimsons, and Electra, canary-yellow ; so that from *R. multiflora* we have already all the best colourings of which Roses are capable, while we may confidently expect many other pretty things.

The name *polyantha* for this Rose is as often given as *multiflora*. It seems needless that the two forms of the specific name should be almost equally in use, the more so that they mean exactly the same thing, *polyantha* being the Greek and *multiflora* the Latin for "many-flowered." Another thing is puzzling to the amateur, that the name *polyantha* is also used for the class of quite dwarf Roses, such as Paquerette, Mignonette, &c. It would seem more sensible to keep the two classes quite apart and to use the name *polyantha* or *multiflora* only for the rambling kinds that retain the free-growing character of the type, and to have for the smaller bushy kinds some simple name that has no pretension to the character of a botanical specific name. A botanical name is in any case wrongly used for any class of garden flower that is a hybrid or a still later cross, and that no-where in nature exists in a single state. These small so-called *polyantha* Roses should be simply called Pompon Roses, then there would be no puzzle or ambiguity, and every one would know what was meant, whereas if Roses fifteen inches and fifteen feet high are both classed as *polyantha*, unless the popular name of each kind is known, there is sure to be confusion.

"It should be remembered that a Rose garden can never be called gorgeous; the term is quite unfitting. Even in high Rose tide, when fullest of bloom, what is most clearly felt is the lovable charm of Rose beauty, whether of the whole scene, or of some delightful detail or incident or even individual bloom. . . here we do not want the mind disturbed or distracted from the beauty and delightfulness of the Rose."

WALTHAM RAMBLER; SINGLE CLUSTER; WHITE AND PINK.

A BRANCH OF THE DOUBLE R POLYANTHA

MADAME ISAAC PÉREIRE (BOURBON) PRUNED AND TRAINED INTO BUSH FORM

These pretty dwarf Cluster Roses are not nearly enough used. They have an innocent, childlike charm of their own, quite distinct from the more grown - up attractiveness of their larger brethren— one thinks of such a little bush as Paquerette as in place in a child's garden or on a child's grave. They have their uses, too, in the Rose garden, in any small, dainty spaces, as at the foot of a platform on which a sundial rests ; at some point where some small beautiful thing could be seen on a level with the eye ; in small beds by themselves, or as an edging to Roses of slightly larger growth.

The Himalayan free Roses have been mentioned first because it is from them, and from *multiflora* especially, that the most important of our newer garden Roses of the rambling, cluster-blooming kinds have been derived. But before coming to some of the older garden Roses, mention must be made of the Japanese *R. wichuriana* and its hybrids. This species has introduced to our gardens Roses of quite an unusual way of growth. They grow fast and are of rambling habit, and though they may be trained to pillar shape, their favourite way is to trail upon the ground, downward as often as not, and to ramble downhill over banks and uneven ground ; so that in our gardens we may now have quite a new aspect of Rose beauty. They hybridise freely, and already we have many beautiful flowers twice the size of the type, more free-blooming, of various tender colourings and charming fragrance. A well - devised cross with Perle des

Jardins (T.) has given us two lovely Roses, Jersey Beauty and Gardenia, of dainty yellow colouring; while Evergreen Gem, whose pollen parent was the pale yellow Tea Madame Hoste, is quite a large flower and deliciously scented. Many a garden has uninteresting turf banks between two levels. Here is one of the most obvious places to use these charming Roses, which are beautiful not only for their blossom, but for the close growth of their neat glossy foliage.

Another Japanese Rose, *R. rugosa*, has also given some valuable varieties and hybrids. The beautiful white Blanc double de Coubert—whitest Rose of any known — has for purity of colour eclipsed the older, duller white Madame Georges Bruant, though this is still indispensable. Blanc double de Coubert is one of the best of Roses, for it blooms the whole summer through and well into autumn. Its rich, deep green foliage, highly polished though heavily reticulated, persisting till late in the year, gives it that look of perfect health and vigour that the leafage of so many Roses lacks in the later summer. The danger in *rugosa* hybrids is the tendency towards a strong magenta colouring, such as is suggested by the type. But in some of the seedlings a judicious choice of pollen parent has amply corrected this, as in the charming salmon-pink Conrad F. Meyer. This, with the white Scheelicht and the pretty white Fimbriata, are among the most charming of the *rugosa* varieties.

The great hardiness of the *rugosas* enables them

ROSA WICHURIANA ON A GRASSY BANK.

MADAME GEORGES BRUANT (RUGOSA); WHITE.

R. RUGOSA SCHNEELICHT; WHITE.

ROSA BRUNONI; WHITE.

to be used in exposed places where many kinds of Roses would be crippled or would perish. Their strong, bushy growth and somewhat ferocious armature of prickles fits them above all other Roses for use as hedges, and not hedges of ornament only, but effective hedges of enclosure and defence.

Among the recent garden Roses of great merit is the beautiful hybrid Tea Dawn, also *Rosa sinica* Anemone, a little tender, but lovely against a wall; while every year is adding to our garden Roses of the loose, half-double Tea class such good things as Sulphurea and Corallina, whose names denote their colourings.

Several beautiful species, formerly in botanical collections only, have also been brought into use, while others have been introduced. Among these are *R. altaica*, described in the chapter on Brier Roses. Then we have *R. macrantha*, with large pink blooms, and *Andersoni*, also with pink flowers; they both make handsome, rather large, bushes. Others of the good wild Roses are dealt with in the chapter on Species as Garden Roses.

The work of the late Lord Penzance among the Sweet Briers has given us a whole range of garden Roses of inestimable value. He sought to give colour and size by means of the pollen parent, and so obtained strong as well as tender colouring and also increased size, while retaining the scented leaf and the free character of growth. It seems as though this eminent lawyer, who in some of the years of his mature practice had to put the law in effect in decreeing the separation of unhappy human couples, had sought mental refreshment in the leisure of his latest days by devoting it to the happy marriages of Roses. Though his name will ever stand high in the records of legal practice, it is doubtful whether in years to come it will not be even more widely known in connection with the Roses he has left us, the fruits of the recreation of his last years of failing strength.

New Garden Roses

R. Brunoni—type, single, milk-white, in clusters.
    Double var.   ,,   ,,
R. Multiflora, *syn. polyantha*—single, white, in large clusters.
    Double   ,,   ,,   ,,
    Large flowered, single   ,,   ,,

Hybrids—
    Crimson Rambler; crimson.
    Euphrosyne; pink.
    Thalia; white.
    Dawson; rose.
    Psyche; pink, salmon-yellow centre.
    Aglaia; yellow-pink.
    Eleanor Berkeley; pale pink.
    Leuchtstern; white and pink.
    Waltham Rambler; white and pink.
    Electra; canary-yellow.
    Claire Jacquier; buff-yellow.
    Queen Alexandra; deep rose-pink, pale centre.
    Lion; single crimson.
    Wallflower; rosy crimson.

Pompon Roses—
    Paquerette; white.
    Anne Marie de Montravel; white.
    Bouquet parfait; light and full rose.
    Eugénie Lamesch; orange, rose-tinted.

THALIA (WHITE RAMBLER).

SULPHUREA. TYPE OF THE NEW LOOSE TEA ROSES
OF BEAUTIFUL COLOURING.

CORALLINA, ONE OF THE NEW LOOSE *TEAS*.

PAUL'S SINGLE WHITE (CLIMBER).

Léonie Lamesch ; copper-red, yellow centre.

Clothilde Soupert ; rose.

Georges Pernet ; rose.

Gloire des Polyantha ; rose and white.

Mignonette ; pale pink.

Mosella ; white and yellow.

Archduchess Elizabeth Marie ; pale yellow.

Clothilde Pfitzer ; white.

R. WICHURIANA—single, white.

HYBRIDS—

Gardenia ; yellow-white.

Jersey Beauty ; single, pale yellow.

Alberic Barbier ; cream-white.

Manda's Triumph ; double, white.

R. RUGOSA—Vars. and Hybrids.

Single, white.

Blanc double de Coubert ; pure white, double.

Madame Georges Bruant ; warm-white.

Fimbriata ; white.

Mercédes ; rose and white.

Souvenir de Philemon Cochet ; white, pink to centre.

Rose Apples ; pink.

SWEET BRIER (*R. rubiginosa*)—

Common, pink.

Double, red.

Janet's Pride ; half-double, striped.

PENZANCE HYBRIDS OF SWEET BRIER, Selection—

Green Mantle ; pink.

Anne of Geierstein ; rose.

Rose Bradwardine ; rose.

Meg Merrilees ; rose.

Lady Penzance ; copper.

VARIOUS—

Rosa sinica Anemone ; pink (tender).

R. moschata nivea ; white.

Others in the chapter on Species as Garden Roses, p. 79.

CHAPTER II

GARDEN ROSES NEW AND OLD

OLD GARDEN ROSES

THE first Rose that comes to mind among the old favourites is the Cabbage or Provence (*R. centifolia*). No Rose surpasses it in excellence of scent; it stands alone as the sweetest of all its kind, as the type of the true Rose smell. The Moss Rose is a variety of the Cabbage Rose, with a mossy calyx having its own delicious scent, of a more aromatic or cordial character. They are so well known that one need say no more than that they should never be neglected or forgotten.

There are several dwarf Roses—dwarf not in the nurseryman's sense, which only means a Rose that is not a standard—but actually dwarf in stature and correspondingly small in all their parts, that are derived from the Provence Rose. These are the neat little De Meaux and the still prettier Spong, and the charming Moss de Meaux, and their white varieties.

Of the old Provins Roses (*R. gallica*) there are a number of catalogued varieties. They are mostly striped or splashed with rosy and purplish colour. I have grown them nearly all, but though certainly

"One of the many ways in which the splendid enthusiasm for good gardening — an enthusiasm which only grows stronger as time goes on — is showing itself, is in the general desire to use beautiful Roses more worthily." Roses planted to grow over trellis work and round the edges of a pool.

RED DAMASK ROSES AND WHITE LILIES.

pretty things, they are of less value in the garden than the striped Damask Rosa Mundi. But there is an old garden Rose, the Blush *gallica*, much more double, and that grows into very strong bushes, that is a good Rose for all gardens. It will put up with any treatment. I have it on the top of a dry wall where it tumbles over in the prettiest way and blooms even more freely than the bushes on the level.

These two names, Provence and Provins, for two classes of garden Roses of the same kind of growth and use, are so much alike that they are one of the puzzles that the Rose amateur has to get clear in his mind in the earlier stages of his education. Provence is the Cabbage Rose (*R. centifolia*); Provins is *Rosa gallica*, the garden kinds being mostly striped; pretty, but not of the first importance; the best as far as my own knowledge and judgment go being Reine Blanche (if it be a true *gallica*) and the full double Blush *gallica*.

Near the Provence Rose, in sentiment as well as in a sort of natural garden classification, comes the Damask, charming also with its delicious though fainter scent and its wide-open crimson flowers. The Damask Rose, with some of the older Gallicas, may be considered the ancestors of many of our modern Roses, and though there is no record of the earlier pedigrees, those who are old enough to remember some of the first Hybrid Perpetuals will retain the recollection of some Roses such as Lee's Perpetual in which such parentage, probably passing through a Portland Rose, of which group there are a few named kinds, is fairly traceable. The parti-coloured form is a charming bush Rose that should be much more used; it is known by the names Rosa Mundi, Cottage Maid, and York and Lancaster. The latter name is also claimed for another striped Rose of much less value, but the name is so pretty and the Rose so charming that most of us think they ought to belong to each other, and that there is at least no harm in their association for gene-ral use.

The newly found but really old garden Rose now called Hebe's Lip, otherwise Reine Blanche, seems to belong to the Provins group (*gallica*). There were formerly in old gardens some very dark-coloured Damask Roses called Velvet Roses, that are either lost or have become rare, as they are now seldom seen.

An old Rose that used to be in nearly every garden and is now but rarely seen is the Cinnamon Rose (*R. cinnamomea*), in some parts of the southern counties called the Whitsuntide Rose. The small flat flowers are pretty and have a distinct scent. It makes a neat bush of rather upright habit. An equally old garden Rose is *R. lucida*, an American species. It is fairly common in old gardens, forming rounded bushes, and will grow anywhere even in the poorest soils, where the autumn tinted foliage, bright yellow and crimson, and the quantities of flat-shaped scarlet hips are very ornamental. The flower is single and of a full pink colour. It seems to like

THE DAMASK ROSE (R. damascena).

THE WHITE ROSE (R. alba), A HALF-DOUBLE FORM.

slight shade, as it shrivels in full sun. There is a strong growing garden variety, much more free in habit than the type, but it does not make such neat bushes. It is remarkable that a Rose so well known should have no English name. The double form that has been long in English gardens, but has never become common, and whose merit is only now becoming recognised, is one of the loveliest of bush Roses. It has the pretty old name Rose d'Amour. How this Rose of American origin first came to be a plant of old English gardens is a question that I must leave to be answered by the botanist-antiquary; what chiefly concerns us is that it is one of the most delightful things in the garden.

The Scotch Briers are considered in the chapter on Brier Roses, and the newer Sweet Briers in that of New Garden Roses, though the old pink single Sweet Brier is, of course, in place here. Many are the ways in which it can be used. Planted in a double row and judiciously pruned, it makes a capital and most fragrant hedge from four to six feet high; but it is perhaps prettiest planted among shrubs, with its graceful arching stems shooting up through them, or in bushy brakes either by itself or among Thorn bushes in one of the regions where the garden joins wilder ground. It will also assume quite a climbing habit if it is led into some tree like a Holly, or encouraged to scramble through straggling Black or White Thorn of tallish growth in some old hedge.

Important among the old garden Roses is *R. alba*. Though it is allowed to bear a botanical name, it is not thought to be a species, but is considered a cross between *canina* and *gallica*. This capital Rose is often seen in cottage gardens, where it is a great favourite. The double white form is the most frequent, but the delicate pink Maiden's Blush is a better flower. Lovelier still is the less double Céleste, a Rose of wonderful beauty when the bud is half opened. When once known the *albas* may be recognised, even out of flower, by the bluish colouring and general look of the very broad leafleted leaves. The blue colouring is accentuated in Céleste, and is a charming accompaniment to the rosy tinting of the heart of the opening flower. The *albas*, as well as others of the garden Roses, make admirable standards, their hardiness and strong constitution enabling them to be grown into quite large-headed bushes. It is no uncommon thing to see standards with heads a yard through in the gardens of cottagers, who also grow some of the Ayrshires in this way.

Rosa alpina has given us the class of free-growing Roses known as Boursault. Of late years so many more and better climbing kinds have been raised, that the Boursaults will probably be less and less used, especially as the crimson varieties of the Amadis type have a rather unpleasant colour. One of this race, the Blush Boursault, would be worthy of a place in every garden if it were not that the flowers are seldom perfect. Every now and then there is a good one, and then it is the loveliest thing in the garden, with its almost matchless tinting of tender milk-white deepening to a wonderfully pure

THE WHITE ROSE (R. alba) ON A COTTAGE PORCH.

A BANK OF PERSIAN AND AUSTRIAN BRIERS IN A SOUTH-COUNTRY GARDEN

rose colour in the centre. Of the others, Morletti, of rather deep pink colouring, is the best. The *alpinas* may be known by their smooth red-barked stems, the mature ones being without prickles. *R. rubrifolia*, with pale pink flowers, red stems and red foliage, is also an *alpina*. In fruit they are conspicuous because of their long-shaped hips.

The field Rose (*R. arvensis*), one of the two of our commonest native hedge Roses (the one with the white, rather clustered flowers), has some good garden varieties. One with large single flowers and strong rambling habit is an old favourite of mine, and another, half double, is equally good and still more free of bloom.

The Banksian Roses (natives of China) are a little tender in England, and are thankful for a place on a warm wall; just such a place as also suits the Persian Briers. The double yellow is the best for growing in England, and lovely it is, with its rich clusters of tiny butter-coloured bloom. In many gardens it is a failure, absolutely refusing to flower, but often does well on chalk soils.

The old Pink China Rose is always welcome, with its pretty clear pink colouring, its dainty scent and neat foliage. It makes compact, low hedges, but I like it best grown with Rosemary bushes. They look just right together and seem to enjoy each other's company. I like to plant them in some place at the foot of a rather warm wall and to train some of the Rosemary to run right up the wall, with other Rosemary bushes free of it in front, and to have it in plenty, and the China Roses sometimes in groups of three or four, sometimes singly and some also trained up the wall among and between the Rosemary bushes.

The crimson China, Cramoisi Supérieur, has long been with us, and also the climbing variety; both capital Roses in their places. There are one or two others of intermediate colouring. But of the old Chinas (garden varieties, not hybrids) the pink and the Cramoisi are the best.

The beautiful Fortune's Yellow has been with us long enough to take its place among the older garden Roses. It is also from China and tender, liking a hot wall; but I have observed that it also likes to be led through some other thin wall shrub that will protect the leaves in May when the late frosts come; this seems to prevent that falling of the leaves in May which so often happens to the unprotected shoots. But it is a Rose that cannot always be trusted to bloom well. We have to consider it a capricious flower. Sometimes it is loaded with its glorious loose copper-coloured bloom, and sometimes it is almost bare. We have to remember that it is from a climate very different from our own, and that we cannot expect to have it in such complete control as we may be fairly sure of assuming in the case of hardier Roses; so that when it does do well we must be all the more thankful.

Coupe d'Hébé, a pretty and sweet Rose of a good full pink colour, is of uncertain origin; it makes a capital pillar Rose. There are also some old Roses

THE LARGE-FLOWERED BANKSIAN ROSE IN A SOUTHERN GARDEN.

AYRSHIRE ROSES IN A KITCHEN GARDEN.

A PILLAR ROSE NEAR WOODLAND,
CLUSTER ROSE, BENNETT'S SEEDLING.

ROSE CELESTIAL.

MADAME PLANTIER, *WHITE*.

A GARDEN FORM OF ROSA ARVENSIS.

of free growth of which Lady Emily Peel and Emilie Plantier are good representatives. Both are of tender colouring and have an interesting, old-world appearance; they bloom in loose bunches—not short-stalked enough to call clusters—but of admirable freedom for cutting in long branches and arranging in water.

SOME OF THE BEST OLD GARDEN ROSES.

CABBAGE OR PROVENCE ROSES (*R. centifolia*).
Other varieties.

MOSS ROSES (*R. centifolia muscosa*)—
Common Pink.
Other varieties.

POMPONS of the *centifolia* class—
De Meaux; pink, and white variety.
Moss de Meaux; pink.
Spong; pink.
Burgundy; pink, and white variety.

PROVINS ROSES (*R. gallica*)—
Mécène; white and rose striped.
Perle des Panachées; white, striped lilac-rose.
Gros Provins Panaché; red and white striped.
Other varieties.

DAMASK (*R. damascena*)—
Common Red.
Cottage Maid, Rosa Mundi, or York and Lancaster; red and white.
One or two other varieties.

CINNAMON ROSE (*R. cinnamomea*); pink.

''We have only to place [rambling roses] well and show them how to go, to lead and persuade them just at the beginning. In two years' time they will understand what is wanted, and will gladly do it of themselves in many ways of their own — ways much better than any that we could possibly have devised.''

R. LUCIDA ; rose.
Rose d'Amour, its double variety.

SCOTCH BRIERS, including the type Burnet Rose (*R. spinosissima*), and the double kinds in several colourings.

SWEET-BRIER, the old single pink.

THE WHITE ROSE (*R. alba*)—
Double White.
Maiden's Blush ; blush.
Celeste ; blush.

BOURSAULT (*R. alpina*)—
Several varieties, the best being—
Morletti ; rose.
Blush Boursault ; blush white, clear rose to centre.

FIELD ROSE (*R. arvensis*) ; white.
Single and half-double garden kinds.

BANKSIAN ROSE (*R. Banksiæ*)—
Double Yellow ; the best, nankeen yellow.

CHINA ROSE (*R. indica*)—
Common Pink.
Cramoisi Supérieur and its climbing variety ; deep crimson.
Other varieties.

FORTUNE'S YELLOW (*R. Fortunei*) ; tender, orange and copper.

MISCELLANEOUS—
Coupe d'Hébé ; pink pillar rose.
Madame Plantier ; white, large bush or pillar.
Emilie Plantier ; free, pink white.
Lady Emily Peel ; free, warm white.
There are other varieties in this class.

PORTLAND ROSES—
Rose du Roi and others ; rose and red.

THE GARLAND ROSE.

CLIMBING CLUSTER ROSES; known as Ayrshire, Hybrids of *sempervirens*, Musk, &c.

Dundee Rambler; warm white.

Garland; warm white.

Bennett's Seedling; white.

Ruga; flesh.

Félicité-Perpétue; cream white

Flora; pink.

Splendens; warm white.

Queen of the Belgians; white.

Some others.

CHAPTER III

THE BRIER ROSES

ROSES of one sort or another are with us in the open garden for five months out of the twelve, namely from the end of May to well on in October.

One of the first to bloom in an ordinary garden collection is likely to be *Rosa altaica*, the close fore-runner of its near relations the Scotch Briers. Though it is a native of a far distant mountain range of Central Asia, it is almost identical in appearance with our native Burnet Rose (*R. spinosissima*). It blooms some ten days earlier and the flowers are a shade larger and the whole plant rather more free of growth, but there is the same bloom of tender lemon white, the same typical brier foliage and the same showy black hips. It is a capital garden plant, and takes its place naturally with the hardy Briers.

By the first week of June the Scotch Briers are in flower, in all their pretty colourings of pink and rose and pale yellow, besides the strongest growing of all, the double white. Those who are interested in this class of Rose should inquire in the good old Scotch gardens, where no doubt fine forms still exist that have not come into trade. One of the best and quite the sweetest has become rare, and sometimes cannot be had even in the best Rose nurseries. It is of a pale

ROSA ALTAICA.

THE BURNET ROSE (R. *spinosissima*) ON A ROUGH GARDEN BANK.

DOUBLE WHITE SCOTCH BRIERS.

PINK SCOTCH BRIERS.

ROSA LUTEA (SPECIES), AND ITS DOUBLE GARDEN VARIETY; BRIGHT YELLOW, 2½ *inches.*

SCOTCH BRIERS.

pink colour, and is conspicuous among other kinds for remaining some time in a globular or half-opened shape. The leaves are of a bluish tint, and the scent is stronger and sweeter than that of any other.

The Scotch Briers are excellent plants for many kinds of use, but are perhaps best of all in wild banks with Heaths and Cistuses. No bushy thing is better for the capping of a dry wall, for it will hang over and also throw out runners between the stones and show itself off quite at its best. These fine hardy Briers have also one merit that most Roses lack, for in winter the leafless crowd of close-growing, plentifully-prickled branches forms masses of warm bronze colouring that have quite a comforting appearance. The pretty Briers might well replace the dull and generally ugly steep slopes of turf that disfigure so many gardens. They are charming accompaniments to steps and their low balustrades ; they are equally in place in the humblest garden and the most exalted, and in all sorts and kinds of places and for all kinds of uses they hardly ever come amiss.

They are also distinctly in place crowning the upper portions of bold rockwork ; in fact this way of having them is one of the very best, for they love free air and unstinted light, and their neat bushy forms and crowded wreaths of bloom are never seen to better advantage than when viewed a little from below.

The Scotch Briers are derived from the native Burnet Rose (*R. spinosissima*), and are amongst the hardiest and most accommodating of their race. Even in the poorest soils they will grow freely if only they are given a little nutritive encouragement in their first year; after that they take care of themselves. The Burnet Rose is found in many parts of England and Scotland, generally in heathy places not very far from the sea. Among its many merits the beauty of its large, round, black hips should not be forgotten. These are like exaggerated black currants, only more flattened at the poles, with a diameter of from half to three-quarters of an inch.

There is a useful Rose, a hybrid of these Briers, that should be grown with them, called Stanwell Perpetual. It fully deserves its name, as it flowers throughout the summer. Its weak point is a somewhat straggly habit. To correct this it is well to place three plants in one group close together—that is to say, about a foot apart—when they will close up and form a well-shaped bush.

We are apt to think of the so-called Austrian Briers in connection with the Scotch, but it should be remembered that whereas the Scotch Briers are among the hardiest of our Roses, the Austrians are rather tender. The name Austrian is misleading, for they are of oriental origin, and except in the most favoured climates of our islands should be in the warmest and most sheltered places we can find for them; but they are so beautiful that they well deserve a good wall space. They are in three or perhaps four forms; the single yellow (*Rosa lutea*), and its double form, the Persian yellow, and another very near garden variety called Harrisoni. Then there is the gorgeous single Austrian Copper, whose petals are yellow outside and vermilion within.

BRIER ROSE, SINGLE YELLOW PERSIAN.

WHITE PET; POMPON.   Flowers under 2 inches across.

CHAPTER IV

POMPON ROSES

SOME mention was made in the chapter on New Garden Roses of the confusion arising from the use of the name *polyantha* for the free rambling kinds, and also for some of the dwarfest growing Roses that we have. The word "dwarf" in Rose language has already been rather erroneously assigned to Roses of bush form to distinguish them from standards, whether the Rose in question will grow twenty feet or only two, so that the name Dwarf Roses would be confusing. Sometimes they are called Miniature Roses, but Pompon is the better name. It is a French word denoting any kind of upholstered ornament of a roundish, tufted form. The name has been excellently applied to the small bloomed Chrysanthemums, whose flowers are about an inch across, and that look like close tufts of petals. Just what Pompon Chrysanthemums are to the other kinds, so are the Pompon Roses to their larger fellows. The most important of them are the small kinds of partly *polyantha* or *multiflora* extraction, with the close, bushy, low-growing habit and clustered flowers.

They are charming plants for any small spaces. They are commonly used as edgings to beds of larger Roses, but it is doubtful whether they are not best by themselves in small beds ; never in large beds, for here the sense of proportion is at once offended. But in a Rose garden, for instance, whose main form would be a long parallelogram, a scheme of some little beds at the ends for the Pompons might be designed with excellent effect, the next group of beds being of kinds of moderate growth, and so on to the larger Roses of the midmost section. Or, in the Rose garden scheme, there may occur some very narrow beds or borders intended to show only as a wide line or single ribbon in the design. Here is the place for the Pompons, and many a little nook in the free garden, and above all in the rock-garden, where they are admirable.

The little Roses de Meaux, Spong, and Moss de Meaux will serve the same use, also the small China Cramoisi Supérieur, and the tiny representatives of the same family known as lawrenceana.

There is also the very charming little Fairy Rose, rarely seen and of doubtful origin, but perhaps the loveliest little Rose, both for its tender colour and for its supreme daintiness, that could well be imagined.

Some of the best POMPONS of the *multiflora* section—
> Amélie Susanne Morin ; white, flushed yellowish.
> Anne Marie de Montravel ; white.
> Archduchess Elizabeth Marie ; canary, buff and white to centre.
> Bouquet parfait ; rose, darker edges.
> Camille de Rochetaille ; white.
> Clara Pfitzer ; silvery white, shaded rose.
> Clothilde Soupert ; rose and red.

"The Rose umbrella [is] a way of training a free-growing standard that, though its evident elaboration of support does not commend it to people of simple taste, yet certainly does produce a wonderful show of bloom."

PERLE D'OR, POMPON.

CUT BRANCHES OF THREE POMPON ROSES

MIGNONETTE, FOMPON, AS A HALF STANDARD.

WHITE PET

Colibri ; copper-yellow, shading to white.
Etoile d'Or ; pale yellow.
Eugénie Lamesch ; buff yellow.
Georges Pernet ; rose, peach and yellow.
Gloire des Polyantha ; rose and white.
Léonie Lamesch ; deep copper-red, yellow centre.
Mosella ; white and yellow.
Mignonette ; pink.
Perle d'Or ; buff yellow.

OTHER POMPON ROSES—
Dwarf *centifolia*, De Meaux.
Moss de Meaux.
Spong.
Lawrenceana and var. Pompon de Paris.
Fairy Rose.
White Pet.
Dwarf Burgundy and white var.

CHAPTER V

SOME OF THE ROSE SPECIES AS GARDEN ROSES

IT is obvious that our garden Roses must have come originally from some wild kinds, and it adds immensely to the interest of our gardens to know something about these original types and the influence they have had in the making of our garden Roses ; moreover some of the actual types are desirable in themselves. Like other classes of plants that are prime favourites, such as Daffodils and Irises, some prominent types have become the ancestors of a host of hybrids and garden varieties, and a close acquaintance with the character of the type plant will often give a very fair idea of the parentage of any garden Rose whose pedigree is unrecorded.

Though Roses have been for many hundred years the most highly prized of garden flowers, yet their antiquity, as far as our modern gardens are concerned, cannot be compared, for instance, to that of wheat, whose origin, in direct association with any one wild grass, has never yet been satisfactorily determined. We can trace the descent of all our Roses, within a move or two, from their wild ancestry, and, by the aid of the eye alone, observe relationships. Botanical characters, such as the strongly serrated stipule in *multiflora*, are a sure guide, but as this book is for

ROSA ALTAICA; LEMON-WHITE, 2½ *to* 3 *inches, and R.* TOMENTOSA
WOODSIANA; PALE LILAC, 1¾ *inches.*

the amateur, and deals with the subjèct from the point of view of garden observation and garden enjoyment, it is well to acquire the more rule-of-thumb, if unscientific, method of noting the visible links. Thus we learn when we see a hybrid Rose whose leaves are bluish and of a dull surface, wide in the leaflet and strongly saw-edged, to at once suspect the influence of *alba*. One soon gets to know the characteristic leaf of a China, and the habit and leaf character of a *centifolia* (Cabbage) or a *gallica*. The leaf of *rugosa*, again, cannot be mistaken, and is strongly shown in its descendants, even though the other parent was some Rose of a very different nature.

There are, of course, a great many species of Roses, and numbers of them are only plants for botanical collections. Only those that concern the garden in the type form, and those that are the parents of garden varieties, are here named and briefly described.

Rosa acicularis.—A Rose with bright pink bloom and glaucous foliage; a native of Siberia; it is pretty and interesting, flowering at the end of May.

R. alba.—Not considered a real species though the name is usually admitted in botanical classification. Semi-double white, with handsome bluish leaves. The double White Rose of cottage gardens, Maiden's Blush and Celeste are among its garden varieties.

R. alpina.—A native of Europe and parent of the Boursault Roses. The mature stems are red and without prickles. The bright red hips are very long in shape.

R. altaica.—The representative of our native Burnet Rose (*R. spinosissima*) in Northern Central Asia. A beautiful garden bush with lemon-white flowers.

R. arvensis.—One of our own hedge Roses; a large single-bloomed variety of extra rambling habit and some half double ones are good garden plants.

R. Banksiæ.—A rambling Chinese Rose without prickles, best known in England by the double yellow form.

R. beggeriana.—From Central Asia; a bush with small glabrous leaves and small, white, unpleasant-smelling flowers; an interesting kind though not showy.

R. blanda.—North American. Called also the Hudson's Bay or Labrador Rose; a good-sized bush with large pink flowers.

R. bracteata.—From China. The Macartney Rose, with large white blooms and handsome polished leaves. There is also a double variety called Marie Léonide which is stronger growing than the type.

R. carolina.—A North American species, not of the first importance, and yet of some value in that it blooms in late summer and autumn.

R. centifolia.—The type of the Cabbage or Provence Roses, of the Moss Roses and the small de Meaux.

R. cinnamomea.—The double form is the Cinnamon Rose of our older gardens. The flowers are rather few, pink or pale rose, and flattened.

R. clynophylla.—A white-flowered trailing Rose of scrambling habit; scarcely suitable for a garden, but good for a wild place.

R. damascena.—(Damask). A good old garden Rose of oriental origin, with several varieties, red, white and striped.

R. Ecæ.—A tender Rose from Abyssinia, with yellow flowers the size of a shilling. It does well occasionally in the south of England.

R. gallica.—The type of most of the older garden Roses. This and the Damask Rose are no doubt the ancestors of the modern Hybrid Perpetuals. Pretty bushes in many varieties.

ROSA ARVENSIS; ONE OF THE WILD ENGLISH ROSES.

ROSA BRACTEATA, THE MACARTNEY ROSE; RATHER TENDER.

ROSA BRUNONI, *syn. MOSCHATA ; WHITE, 2 inches.*

ROSA HISPIDA, NEARLY ALLIED TO R. SPINOSISSIMA; PALE LEMON, 2½ inches.

ROSA MACRANTHA (Natural hybrid); PALE PINK, 3½ inches, AND PAUL'S SINGLE SCARLET; SCARLET, 3 inches.

*R. CALOCARPA, A FORM OF R. RUGOSA, AND R. HUMILIS RUGOSA.
BOTH MAGENTA-PINK,* 3½ *inches.*

R. humilis.—A white Rose. *R. humilis rugosa* is an excellent bush garden Rose with pink flowers.

R. indica.—The type of the China Rose, but there are other forms of *R. indica* that are apparently the types of some of the Teas.

R. lævigata.—A native of China; it makes a good pillar or climbing Rose in the south of England, though it is better in France. It has shining leaves and large white flowers.

R. lucida.—A well-known garden Rose from North America, with shining leaves and rose-coloured flowers. It grows into bushy masses. The double variety, though not common, is very beautiful.

R. lutea.—An oriental yellow Brier, the origin of the double Persian yellow, and of the Austrian Copper.

R. macrantha.—Single large rose coloured; a wild hybrid of *canina* and *gallica.*

R. macrophylla.—A handsome, tall growing Rose with many large, full-pink flowers. It makes a good pillar Rose and deserves to be more generally planted.

R. microphylla.—A Chinese Rose with buff-coloured wood and straight, sharp, gooseberry-like prickles. The bud is curious from the prickly calyx. The double variety is a handsome flat flower, light pink, with crimson centre.

R. mollis pomifera.—The Apple-bearing Rose of older gardens. The foliage is soft and bluish, the flowers pink and the hips large and handsome.

R. moschata = R. Brunoni.—A rambling Himalayan Rose of great beauty, bearing a quantity of clustered white bloom and having graceful bluish foliage. Best used to ramble through trees and bushes.

R. multiflora = polyantha.—Of eastern Asiatic origin. It makes large bushy brakes by itself and is the parent of many of our best rambling Roses.

R. omissa.—An erect bush with pink flowers and grey, softly pubescent leaves. A pretty and interesting Rose.

R. pisocarpa.—A rather straggling Californian bush, flowering in corymbs. The leaves are glabrous and the flowers pink or red.

R. Pissardi.—A handsome Persian Rose with white bloom.

R. rubiginosa.—The native Sweet-brier. In the type form an indispensable Rose. The beautiful Penzance hybrids derived from it should be in every garden.

R. rugosa.—The Japanese Ramanas Rose. One of the hardiest of Roses. There are good garden forms and hybrids. The hips are the showiest of any known Rose.

R. rubrifolia.—An European Rose with small red flowers and red stems and leaves ; very near *R. alpina.*

R. sempervirens.—A wild Italian Rose, the parent of many of our older cluster and rambling Roses. The leaves are small and polished and endure through the greater part of the winter.

R. setigera.—The latest to bloom of the wild Roses. From North America. Flowers magenta-rose. It makes a good pillar Rose.

R. simplicifolia = berberifolia.—A small and tender yellow Rose, requiring a sheltered place against a warm wall.

R. spinosissima.—The native Burnet Rose, type of the well-known Scotch Briers.

R. wichuriana. — A trailing Japanese species with small, polished, deep green leaves and white flowers. Beautiful hybrids are now being derived from it.

THE BURNET ROSE (R. spinosissima) ; LEMON-WHITE.

Writing of the arbour, Gertrude Jekyll commented that, whatever form it takes, ''some free Roses at its opening offer a charming invitation to enter and rest in grateful shade in the June and July days of their blooming season.''

CHAPTER VI

ROSES ON THEIR OWN ROOTS

MANY of our ordinary garden Roses are necessarily own root plants. This is because they are so easily propagated by other methods than budding. Provence, Damask, the albas and the Briers increase by suckers, Sweet-brier by seed or cuttings, and the free-growing Ayrshires and multiflora hybrids by cuttings or layers. But there are many gardens where other Roses, especially the Teas and Hybrid Teas, kinds that with rare exceptions are sold grafted, would be better on their own roots.

Such plants have several advantages. They are much longer lived, they give more bloom, they bloom more continuously, and they throw up no troublesome suckers.

The common Dog Rose, the most usual stock in England, is very troublesome in the way of suckers, and often in the case of Roses from some good foreign raiser, the stock, if not carefully watched, will overpower the scion, and we find we have a flourishing bush certainly, but of Manetti or of De la Grifferaie instead of the Rose desired.

Grafted plants may be best for the production of show blooms, but the bush that is to produce the show bloom is to a great extent reared and nurtured for that purpose, and the severe pruning to encourage larger flowers and the shading to preserve colour put the plant that is to bear them out of the category of beautiful things in the garden, whereas the own root Roses, bearing slightly smaller flowers—though there are exceptions even to this—fulfil their best purpose as true garden plants.

There can be no doubt that on rather light soils and quite poor ones—not of course left to themselves, but moderately and reasonably improved—own root Roses of the kinds classed as show Roses do better than grafted. This being so, and their other advantages being considered, it seems strange that they are not oftener so grown. Moreover they strike readily in July and August, so that if they cannot be obtained elsewhere, they can easily be made at home from grafted plants.

Every one who has grown Roses on a poor or dry soil, even when beds have been well prepared and duly mulched and all reasonable care given, knows only too well that sad, worn-out look of unhappy grafted Roses, some three years after planting. There are varieties that to the Rose lover are indispensable, such as Catherine Mermet, a kind that will do quite well in such soils on its own roots, whereas the same grand Rose grafted is a total failure.

There is also a satisfaction in knowing just what one is growing. If a Rose is on its own roots there is no doubt about its identity. If it fails after reasonable trial we may know that the Rose itself will not be happy, and not that it is perhaps a

SOME OF THE FREE-GROWING ROSES ON THEIR OWN ROOTS.

DUNDEE RAMBLER (*Ayshire*), ON ITS OWN ROOTS.

tantrum of the stock—maybe we do not even know what stock!

Then the foreign stocks are plants from various parts of Europe, perhaps from soils of quite different chemical constituents. Some particular stock may not suit some particular garden, so that the grower's perplexities are much increased, and he is offered additional chances of going wrong. If the plant is on its own roots and fairly treated it does well or it does not, and there the matter ends.

FREE CLUSTER ROSES ON THEIR OWN ROOTS.

GLOIRE LYONNAISE (*H.T.*)

CHAPTER VII

ROSE PILLARS

A PILLAR in garden phrase is rather an elastic term, for though a Rose pillar pure and simple is what it seems to be—that is to say, a Rose grown to a certain height in upright shape—there are other developments of the form that are commonly accepted as of the pillar family, and may be conveniently described under the same title. The foundation of the pillar proper is generally a post of larch or oak or a narrow upright iron framework. A Rose is chosen whose height and natural way of growth is suitable, and it is trained and encouraged to grow so that it will show a column of bloom over the greater part of its surface, and so as not to be too leggy at the bottom. A perspective of Rose pillars is a charming feature in a garden, and one of the ways in which their beauty may be best enjoyed. They should be so placed that one can go right up to them and see the Roses at eye level and below it and also against the sky, and smell their sweet scent in perfect comfort as they grow. The posts may either stand quite free, or, for the better showing of the rambling Roses, be connected by a chain that hangs in easy festoons.

Another form of pillar is of greater width, when either three or four posts are planted in group, or a

GLOIRE LYONNAISE (H T) IN A SOUTHERN GARDEN.

AYRSHIRE ROSE ON PILLAR.

A PILLAR ROSE IN THE FREE GARDEN.

QUEEN ALEXANDRA (RAMBLER), PINK WITH DEEPER CENTRE.

SIX PLANTS OF CLIMBING AIMÉE VIBERT (N.),
BALLOON-TRAINED ON IRON ARCHES.

*SIX PLANTS OF BENNETT'S SEEDLING (Ayrshire),
BALLOON-TRAINED ON IRON ARCHES.*

A STRONG STANDARD DUNDEE RAMBLER (Ayrshire), UMBRELLA TRAINED.

wider iron frame is placed to make a thicker block of upright Roses. Another is wider still, and the Roses are trained either up or round it outside, or up a central support and then out at the top, from whence they fall over and cover the sides. This is an excellent way of growing that beautiful old Rose Blairii No. 2. For full fifty years this fine thing has been with us, and in its own way there is as yet nothing better. Its origin is not clearly known, but it seems to be related to the China Roses. Its dainty pink colouring, deepening to the centre, gives it a rare charm, and recalls the loveliness of a looser Rose, the Blush Boursault, that, alas ! so seldom gives well-formed blooms. Another way of forming the thick pillar or balloon is to have a stout wooden central post and three intersecting iron arches each six feet wide, forming six outer standards that arch over to the central post, and lateral wires girthing the whole about eighteen inches apart. The post should be five to six inches thick, the iron arches three-eighths of an inch, and the lateral wires one-quarter inch. In the case of a structure of this size six plants of the same kind of Rose are used, one to each upright, and all are trained upwards.

This thick form of pillar leads to the Rose umbrella, a way of training a free-growing standard that, though its evident elaboration of support does not commend it to people of simple taste, yet certainly does produce a wonderful show of bloom. But the iron frame, if of any size, has to be guyed all round by stiffly strained wires, and these have to be fixed to stumps

"*A perspective of Rose pillars is a charming feature in a garden, and one of the ways in which their beauty may be best enjoyed. They should be so placed that one can go right up to them and see the Roses at eye level and below it and also against the sky, and smell their sweet scent in perfect comfort as they grow.*" *Rosa Chaplin's Companion.*

driven into the ground, and some of us feel that a way of growing that entails the necessity of employing such complicated machinery of support is out of harmony with the Rose sentiment and damping to Rose fervour.

SOME OF THE BEST PILLAR ROSES (TALL).

Multiflora hybrids (see p. 72).
Wichuriana hybrids (see p. 35).
Ayrshires (see p. 59).
Climbing Aimée Vibert, N. ; white.
Waltham Climber, T. ; red.
Reine Marie Henriette, H.T. ; rosy red.
Reine Olga de Wurtemburg, H.T. ; red.
Carmine Pillar, Hyb. ; deep rose.
Crimson Rambler, Mult. ; crimson.
Longworth Rambler, N. ; rose-crimson.
Gloire de Dijon, T. ; buff and orange.
Bouquet d'Or, T. ;   ,,   ,,
Madame Bérard, T. ;   ,,   ,,
Penzance Briers (see p. 35).
William Allen Richardson, N. ; orange.
Madame Alfred Carrière, H.N. ; warm white.
Bardou Job, T. ; dark red.
Baronne de Hoffmann, T. ; copper red.
Climbing Devoniensis, T. ; yellow white.
Clothilde Soupert, T. ; carmine rose.
Duchesse D'Auerstadt, T. ; yellow.
Fanny Stolwerk, T. ; salmon rose.
Pink Rover, H.T. ; light rose.
Paul's Single White.
Ard's Rover, H.P. ; red.

ROSE PILLARS IN A FLOWER BORDER.

PAUL'S CARMINE PILLAR, SCARLET CRIMSON, 3 *inches.*

SOME PILLAR ROSES OF MODERATE HEIGHT.

Purity, H.B.; white.
Belle Lyonnaise, T.; buff white.
Alister Stella Gray, N.; buff.
Climbing Captain Christy, H.C.; blush and pink.
Climbing Mrs. W. J. Grant, H.T.; salmon pink.
Climbing Kaiserin Augusta Victoria, H.T.; white shaded
    to centre.
Gloire Lyonnaise, H.T.; white, lemon centre.
Grüss an Teplitz, H.T.; crimson.
Dawn, H.T.; nearly single, pale pink.
Coupe d'Hébé, Hyb.; pink.
Madame Plantier, Hyb.; white.
Blairii No. 2, Hyb.; clear pink and pink white.
Climbing Eugénie Verdier, H.P.; salmon pink.
Brightness of Cheshunt, H.P.; red.
Frances Bloxam, H.C.; salmon pink.
Climbing Victor Verdier, H.P.; red.
Climbing Pride of Waltham, H.P.; salmon.
Gloire des Rosomanes, Hyb.; red.
Charles Lawson, H.P.; rose.

CHAPTER VIII

THE PERGOLA

EVERY garden is now wanting a Pergola, that pleasant shape of covered way that we have borrowed from Italy, where it is employed not only for its grateful shade but because it is just the right kind of support and way of treatment for the vines of sunny southern lands.

We have adopted the name because it is more convenient than the older name of covered alley, which three centuries ago was its nearest equivalent in English gardens. But this was formed on a much more elaborate wooden framework, a kind of uninterrupted arched trellis for the training of some green tree such as Hornbeam or Wych Elm, whose rigid branches had to be closely watched and carefully guided and fixed until the whole covering was complete; after which the chief care was the outer clipping into shape.

The modern pergola is a more free thing altogether and differently constructed. Upright piers of brick, stone, iron or wood are erected in pairs across the path and a connecting beam is put in place. A slighter top is made with thinner pieces such as larch poles, and the whole is planted with free growing climbers.

CLUSTER ROSES ON A PERGOLA.

A WELL-PLACED PERGOLA, DIVIDING TWO GARDEN SPACES.

A Rose pergola should be so placed that it is well seen from the sides. One whose purpose is merely to make a shady way is better covered with leafy growths of Vine, Aristolochia or Virginia Creeper, for if they have not free air and space at the sides, the Roses will merely rush up and extend skyward where they cannot be seen.

But a pergola that crosses some open grassy space, such as might divide two portions of a garden, or that forms a middle line in the design of one complete garden scheme, is admirably suited for Roses, and a broad turf walk on each side will allow them to be seen to the best advantage.

Here it may be well to observe that a structure such as this, which is of some importance of size and appearance, cannot just be dabbed down anywhere. It ought to lead distinctly from some clear beginning to some definite end ; it should be a distinct part of a scheme, otherwise it merely looks silly and out of place. If there is no space where it will be clearly right it is better not to have it. There are arrangements less binding to definite design, such as pillars of Roses or arches at a cross walk, and many free uses on fences, trees, and unsightly places. An arboured seat is always a good ending to a pergola, and a place where ways meet often suggests a suitable beginning. Such a place may be glorified by circular or octagonal treatment, with a central tank or fountain, and pillars of Roses to mark the points of the octagon or relative points on the circumference. But space, proportion, and the nature of the environment must all be considered; indeed in this, as in the very smallest detail of procedure in garden design, just the right thing should be done or it is better let alone.

In small gardens in which there is no general design there often occurs some space where one department gives place to another—as when flower garden adjoins vegetable ground—where a short pergola-like structure of two or three pairs of posts may be quite in place and will form a kind of deepened archway. Such an arrangement in iron is shown on page 116, where it makes a pleasant break in an awkward corner where there is a mixture of wall and flower border and a turn of the path.

The pergola proper should be always on a level and should never curl or twist. If a change of level occurs in its length in the place where it is proposed to have it, it is much better to excavate and put in a bit of dry wall right and left and steps at the end, either free of the last arch or with the last two pairs of piers carried up square to a higher level, so as to give as much head-room at ·the top step as there is in the main alley.

There is a great advantage in having solid piers of masonry for such structures; piers of fourteen-inch brickwork are excellent, and in some districts even monoliths of stone can be obtained; but often the expense of stone or brickwork cannot be undertaken and something slighter and less costly must be used. The illustration of a Wistaria pergola (page 121) is instructive because the structure shown is only a few

"A Rose pergola should be so placed that it is well seen from the sides. . . One that crosses some open grassy space, such as might divide two portions of a garden, or that forms a middle line in the design of one complete garden scheme, is admirably suited for Roses, and a broad turf walk on each side will allow them to be seen to the best advantage."

PERGOLA WITH SOLID BRICK PIERS. ROSE FÉLICITÉ-PERPÉTUE;
2½ years after planting.

*PERGOLA OF LIGHT SQUARED WOOD POSTS
ON STONE BASES.*

"What a splendid exercise it would be if people would only go round their places and. . . think how they might be made beautiful by the use of. . . Roses." Rosa xamadis and Rosa indica var. growing round a garden gateway.

years old and the way the framework is made may be clearly seen.

Here it is of squared wood, with the beams partly supported and much strengthened, and the whole fabric stiffened, by slightly curved or cambered braces of the same. It should be noticed how much the curve of the brace adds to the strength of the support and how pleasantly it satisfies the eye. It would have been better still if the beam itself had been ever so slightly cambered. It will also be seen that the feet of the posts, instead of going into the ground, rest on a wrought stone; an iron dowel let into both stone and post fixing it firmly. Thus there is no danger of the foot of the post rotting.

For the first year or two there is no need to fill in the top with the slighter poles that later will support the more extensive growths of the creepers; indeed the whole thing is very pretty, with a different kind of form and beauty, to the mature pergola with its fully filled roof. In these earlier years one sees more of the individual plants, and their first vigour of growth and bloom can be more fully enjoyed. In many cases such pairs of posts with connecting beam and side rails, but without roof, are more suitable than the complete pergola. This arrangement is shown in the pictures where they are placed across the main walks of the kitchen garden and where the Roses are to be seen from the walk alone, not from the sides, which are only vegetable quarters.

In some of the illustrations the framework is of the simplest possible construction, of oak or of larch. In

ROSE FLORA ON PERGOLA OF ROUGH LARCH.

A ROSE PERGOLA OF ROUGH OAK

ROSA BRUNONI ON THE OUTSIDE OF A PERGOLA.

A ROSE PERGOLA OF ROUGH LARCH DIVIDING KITCHEN GARDEN QUARTERS.

HANGING GARLANDS ON A ROSE PERGOLA.

THE LARGE-FLOWERED BANKSIAN ROSE IN A SOUTHERN GARDEN.

ROSA ARVENSIS AND AYRSHIRES OUTSIDE A PERGOLA OF ROUGH OAK.

A PERGOLA OVER A GRASS WALK.

these the posts go into the ground. This of course will have a shorter lifetime, and after several years signs of weakness must be looked for. A spur of larch or oak going deep into the ground and nailed or bolted to a shaky post will prolong its life for some more years, but there always comes a time of sore regret (when constant repair is needed) that it was not made more structurally permanent at the beginning.

The sides of the pergola may be much ornamented by hanging garlands of Roses trained to chains.

"Many are the opportunities in the planning of gardens for having a screen or hedge all of Roses. Sometimes it may occur as part of the Rose garden design, but more often in some detached portion of the grounds some kind of light screen is actually wanted."

A RANGE OF ROSE ARCHES

A ROSE PERGOLA OF IRON FRAMEWORK.

FÉLICITÉ-PERPÉTUE ON AN ARCH OVER A GARDEN PATH.

CHAPTER IX

ROSE ARCHES AND ARBOURS

MANY are the ways in which an arch of Roses may be beautiful in the garden, whether it be a garden of some distinctly set design or one that is quite informal.

Where two ways meet or cross at a right angle there is always an opportunity for the placing of an arch of Roses, or where flower garden passes into kitchen garden, whether it be walled or not. A Rose arch is none the less a Rose arch because there is a brick arch behind it, although what is generally understood as a Rose arch is one that stands free or is in connection with a bounding hedge, the Rose itself forming the arch, only supported by a framework of wood or iron.

But often in a modest garden there are other uses for a Rose arch, such as the garden will itself suggest. For instance, where a double flower border is made in a kitchen garden, and it is desirable to take up as little space as may be, a whole Rose scheme may be conveniently combined with borders of useful flowers for cutting or for contemplation. A four-foot grass or gravel path would have on each side borders of five feet wide. At intervals of twenty-five feet, Rose arches, the foot of the arches planted in the back

CRIMSON RAMBLER OVER A GARDEN HAND-GATE

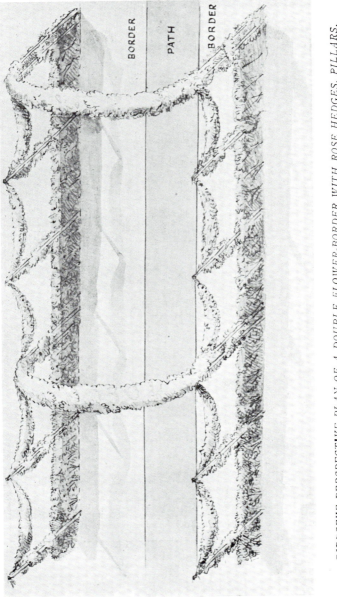

BORDER

PATH

BORDER

BIRDSEYE PERSPECTIVE PLAN OF A DOUBLE FLOWER-BORDER WITH ROSE HEDGES, PILLARS, ARCHES, &c., as described on page 137 of the borders, span the whole. At the back of both borders is a hedge of Roses that will grow about three feet high. If the space is divided into four, points will be found for three pillar Roses rising from the hedge and in a line with it ; those will therefore stand about eight feet apart.

The illustration shows a Crimson Rambler trained over a wire support in a free hedge of Rhododendrons in a place where a path from one division of a garden leads into another (p. 138).

An incident in this picture that is not at all of unfrequent occurrence is worthy of notice. It is the carefully made rabbit-proof iron fencing, with two wires out in the lower part of the gate, leaving a space which seems to invite the entrance of any small animal. When it is desired to keep out rabbits, and an expensive fence is put up for the purpose, one such oversight makes the whole thing useless. Gates of this slight construction, which are in themselves perhaps the least distressing to the eye of all their unsightly class, are especially liable to injury from an accidental kick, or a blow from a barrow wheel.

Wrought iron gates, with richly designed ornament of the best kind that are made for the place itself, of perfect proportion and suitable enrichment, may well lead into and out of the Rose garden, or indeed any other garden division, and Roses may clamber near them, but it is more fitting that they should not climb over or into gates or screens of this class. Two such richly decorated objects as the artist-craftsman's work in enduring metal and the clusters of living Rose had

"An arch of Roses may be beautiful in the garden, whether it be a garden of some distinctly set design or one that is quite informal. . .there is always an opportunity for the placing of an arch of Roses."

AYRSHIRE ROSE ON AN ARCH IN KITCHEN GARDEN WALL.

ROSE ARCHES CONNECTING A WALL-BORDER, LAWN AND FLOWER-GARDEN.

better be seen and enjoyed separately. But in the case of a simple arch in a brick garden wall and a wrought-iron gate of very simple design, such as the one in the illustration, the Rose is a welcome and rightly placed addition to the garden picture. The simple old Rose arbour, by no means so often seen as it might well be, should be in every modest garden. A Dundee Rambler on one side to cover the top, and an Aimée Vibert, or an *alba* kept to pillar height, to clothe the other side, will be an ample furnishing, though there is a sense of additional comfort if the back wall, unless the arbour is actually against a wall of brick or stone, were of some solid greenery, such as yew or box. An arbour may be anything between this and a more important structure, but in any case some free Roses at its opening offer a charming invitation to enter and rest in grateful shade in the June and July days of their blooming season.

Often in a modest garden there are. . . uses for a Rose arch, such as the garden will self suggest. For instance, where. . . it is desirable to take up as little space as may be, whole Rose scheme may be conveniently combined with borders of useful flowers for tting or for contemplation.''

DUNDEE RAMBLER ON A GARDEN GATEWAY.

CLUSTER ROSE FÉLICITÉ-PERPÉTUE ON A GARDEN ARCH.

A WIDE ARCH IN A ROSE GARDEN.

DUNDEE RAMBLER (Ayrshire), ON A GARDEN ARCH,

CHAPTER X

MANY are the opportunities in the planning of gardens for having a screen or hedge all of Roses. Sometimes it may occur as part of the Rose garden design, but more often in some detached portion of the grounds some kind of light screen is actually wanted. There are often rubbishy or at least unbeautiful spaces on some of the frontiers of the kitchen garden, where a Rose screen or hedge will not only hide the unsightliness, but will provide a thing beautiful in itself and that yields a large quantity of bloom for cutting. Many are the kinds of structure that may be used to support and train the Roses. But with posts of oak or larch, and straight long lengths of sawn larch tips for the top rail, and some wire netting of the coarsest mesh, an effective framework may be easily and cheaply made that in three years will show a perfect covering of blooming Roses. Between this and the elaborately made wooden framings there are many grades and forms of flower wall or trellis that can be arranged according to special use or need. One pretty way is to have a low trellis with posts for pillar Roses at intervals. This can be carried a little further by having chains from post to post. If this should occur on each side of a path, the posts

A ROSE SCREEN.

WILLIAM ALLEN RICHARDSON (Noisette), ON A FENCE.

coming opposite each other can be connected by an arched top. This arrangement can also be very prettily adapted to such a Rose trellis at the back of a flower border, either at the two ends of the border or at intervals in its length. It would be an extremely pretty way of having a double flower border in three divisions, with such an open cross screen twice in the length, as well as at the beginning and end. The first division of the border might well be flowers all blue and white and pale yellow, with bluish foliage ; the middle one of warm colourings of rose, red, scarlet, orange, and full yellows, and the third of purple, pale pink and white flowers, with silvery and other cool foliage.

Chains are generally used to form the garlands from post to post, and they are the best, as they hang in a good natural line. A cheaper and not bad substitute is wire rope. Whether chain or rope is used it is an excellent plan, and much better for the Roses, to wind thick tarred twine, or something stronger than twine — tarred cord as thick as the diameter of a large Sweet Pea seed — round and round the chain or wire, keeping the coils rather close, so that the Rose branches do not actually touch the iron but rest upon the coiled cord.

For the post and low trellis the posts are planted with any of the good ramblers or Roses of free growth, while the low trellis may have strong growing H.P.s or any of the Teas and Hybrid Teas usually described in Rose lists as " vigorous." In this case two Roses, or three, according to space,

"Roses of the free-growing kinds adapt themselves readily to the form of hedges. One has only to choose a Rose of more or less vigour, according to the height required. The hedge or screen way of growing them has the merit of ease of access for training and pruning as well as that of giving close enjoyment of the living walls of flowers." A hedge of Albertine and Zephirin Drouhin.

preferably of the same kind, would be planted against each panel of the trellis. Another way would be to plant another Rose of rambling habit against the middle of the trellis and train it down over its next neighbour.

Posts when put into the ground should always have the ends prepared either by gas-tarring or by charring in the fire. This preparation should come up the post quite a foot out of the ground, as damp and rot attack it first at or near the ground line. If a better kind of wooden framework is made, the posts are set on stone or brickwork nine inches to a foot out of the ground, as described in the chapter on the pergola on p. 114.

Roses of the free-growing kinds adapt themselves readily to the form of hedges. One has only to choose a Rose of more or less vigour, according to the height required. The hedge or screen way of growing them has the merit of ease of access for training and pruning as well as that of giving close enjoyment of the living walls of flowers. The tendency of nearly all strong growing Roses is to rush up and leave bare places below. A Rose hedge should, if possible, have a free space on both sides, when this defect can be remedied in two ways; one by training the shoots in an arched form with the tips bent well down, and the other to tip some of the outer strong young shoots that spring from the base. If in July these are shortened about a third, instead

A HEDGE OF PINK ROVER (H.T.)

A HEDGE OF PSYCHE (Rambler).

PART OF AN OPEN ROSE SCREEN.

of continuing their growth in length, their energy goes to strengthening the shortened piece that is left. This will then, the following season, be thickly set with flowering laterals that will clothe the lower part of the hedge.

Many of the newer rambling Roses, the old Ayrshires and the stronger of the Teas, are admirable for this way of growth, while there are Roses to suit every height. The height of the Rose hedge, as in all other matters of garden design, must be determined in relation to the proportion of the space it is to fill and the size and distribution of whatever may be within view. Nothing is gained by carrying it up to a great height. Eight or nine feet is in most cases the limit of desirable height, while anything from four to seven feet will be likely to suit the wants of most modest gardens. A charming hedge four feet high can be made with the old favourite Madame Plantier. It is all the prettier if there is a short standard of the same at regular intervals. Another pretty hedge of the same class can be made with this good Rose in combination with one of pink colouring, such as the old H.P. Anna Alexieff. I know a pretty Rose hedge where the two are mixed ; not planted alternately, but two or three of one kind and then one of the other, and so on in irregular sequence. Or it would be charming to have short standards of Anna Alexieff rising as just described from the low hedge of the white Madame Plantier.

No one would regret some planting of these two excellent old garden Roses. This one example is given as a type of this kind of planting. Any one who tried it and had enough garden sensibility to feel its charm, and enough garden fervour to wish to practise it in varied forms, would soon invent other combinations.

It would be easy to name many such desirable mixtures, but it is more helpful to show one simple thing that is easily understood, and that awakens interest and enthusiasm, and to leave those wholesome motive powers to do their own work, than it is to prompt the learner at every step, fussing like an anxious nurse, and doing for him, what, if his enthusiasm is true and deep and not mere idle froth, will give him more pleasure in the doing, and more profit in the learning, than if it were all done for him. For the very essence of good gardening is the taking of thought and trouble.   No one can do good decorative work who does it merely from a written recipe. The use of such a book as this is to describe enough to set the Rose pilgrim on his road, not to blindfold him and lead him all the way by hand.

MADAME ALFRED CARRIÈRE (N.) GROWN AS A HEDGE.

THE GARLAND ROSE IN A COTTAGE GARDEN.

CHAPTER XI

AMONG the many ways of worthily using the free Ayrshire Roses, one of the best is to leave them to their own way of growth, without any staking or guiding whatever. Due space must be allowed for their full size, which will be a diameter of some ten feet. Of these useful garden Roses none is more beautiful than the Garland, with its masses of pretty blush-white bloom. It is well worth getting up at 4 A.M. on a mid-June morning to see the tender loveliness of the newly opening buds; for, beautiful though they are at noon, they are better still when just awaking after the refreshing influence of the short summer night.

Several others among the old Ayrshires are excellent in this way of growth, though perhaps there are none to beat the Garland and Dundee Rambler. A grassy space where they may be seen all round, or a place where the great bush may be free at least on two sides, are the most suitable, or they may be used as central or symmetrically recurring points in a Rose garden of some size. The young growths that show above the mass when the bloom is waning are the flowering branches of next year; they will arch over and bear the clusters of flowers on short stems thrown out at each joint. The way these young main branches spring up and bend over when mature is exactly the way that best displays the bloom. Each little flower of the cluster is shown in just the most beautiful way ; and it is charming to see, when light winds are about, how the ends of the sprays, slightly stirred by the active air, make pretty curtseying movements arising from the weight of the crowded bloom and the elasticity of the supporting stem.

There is a whole range of use of these beautiful Roses, from this free fountain shape without any artificial support, to association with trees and bushes in shrub clumps and wood edges, and from that to clambering into the trees themselves.

The illustration shows this pretty Cluster Rose growing over and among some Pernettyas, beside a broad grassy way that passes from garden into copse. The young growths may be seen rising above it, as yet quite soft and tender, and only half grown. As the year goes on they will harden and mature and arch over, and next year bloom in their turn.

When these free Roses rush up into trees, instead of throwing out their new growths from close to the earth, they are formed upon the older wood higher up, and the stem or stems that supports them go on growing till sometimes they attain a considerable thickness.

Everything that has been said of the Garland Rose, as to its use as a fountain Rose or free climber, may also be said of Dundee Rambler, Bennett's Seedling, Félicité-Perpetue, and others of the cluster Roses

THE GARLAND ROSE IN THE GARDEN LANDSCAPE.

ROSE FLORA (Evergreen Cluster), GROWING INTO SHRUBS.

CLUSTER ROSE (*Sempervirens*) *AS A BUSH*.

CLIMBING AIMÉE VIBERT (N.) RAMBLING OVER WILLOWS

classed as Ayrshires. They are all worthy of use in these ways, and of being encouraged to clamber into trees and hedges. One cannot help observing how the support of a tree encourages almost abnormal growth. The wild Dog-rose will go up twenty feet, and Sweet-brier nearly as high; while almost any Rose that has at all a climbing habit will exert itself to the utmost to get high up into the tree.

Climbing Aimée Vibert is generally used as a pillar Rose, but the picture shows how it will rush up into a tree and increase, not only in height but in freedom of flowering.

The free-growing *R. multiflora* of the Himalayas also forms immense fountains, spreading in diameter by naturally rooted layers, from which new plants take root at the outer circumference of the great bush, throwing up strong growths, and so continually increasing its area. The large flowered one (*R. multiflora grandiflora*), as well as the double kind, are valuable varieties, with all the freedom of the type, while each has its own distinct development of somewhat the same class of beauty.

For spaces between garden and wild, for sloping banks, for broken ground, as of an old gravel pit or other excavation, for all sorts of odds and ends of unclassified places about the home grounds, the rambling and free-growing Roses seem to be offered us by a specially benevolent horticultural providence. A well-prepared hole is all they need at first. About four years after planting, if the best they can do for us is desired, they should be looked to in the way of removing old wood. This should be done every two years, but beyond this they need no pruning and no staking whatever. When they begin to grow freely among bushes or trees, if it is desired to lead the far-reaching growths one way rather than another, it is easily done with a long forked stick, and a very pleasant and interesting job it is. It is like painting a picture with an immensely long-handled brush, for with a fourteen-foot pole with a forked end one can guide the branches into Yew or Holly or tall Thorn very nearly into such forms of upright spring or downward swag as one pleases.

It is pleasant, too, in such rough places, to see the behaviour of one of these Roses on the ground without support, and to watch the different way of its own brother plant climbing into a neighbouring tree.

Of roses one may leave to their own way of growth, Gertrude Jekyll wrote: "A grassy space where they may be seen all round, or a place where the great bush may be free at least on two sides, are the most suitable. . . . The way. . . young main branches spring up and bend over when mature is exactly the way that best displays the bloom. Each little flower of the cluster is shown in just the most beautiful way; and it is charming to see, when light winds are about, how the ends of the sprays, slightly stirred by the active air, make pretty curtseying movements arising from the weight of the crowded bloom and the elasticity of the supporting stem." Rosa Gallica Pompon de Bourgogne.

THE GARLAND ROSE RAMBLING OVER A YEW

THE GARLAND ROSE IN AN OLD CATALPA.

ROSA MULTIFLORA, syn. Polyantha, ON A BANK.

ROSES AND CISTUSES IN THE ROCK-GARDEN. IN THE
LOWER LEFT HAND CORNER CISTUS HIRSUTUS ; IN
THE MIDDLE ROSA ALBA ; TO THE RIGHT R.
RUGOSA var. MADAME GEORGES BRUANT.

A BRANCH OF DUNDEE RAMBLER.

ROSE FLORA ON A GARDEN HOUSE.

CLIMBING AIMÉE VIBERT BY A COTTAGE DOOR

CHAPTER XII

ROSES ON WALLS AND HOUSES

THE name Cluster Rose, which formerly belonged almost entirely to the older class of garden Roses known as the Ayrshires, varieties of *sempervirens*, and the Musk Roses, has lately been necessarily extended to all the beautiful things that the last few years have given us, most of them hybrids of *Rosa multiflora* or *polyantha*. All these Roses are derived from species of rambling habit that in their native places climb about among rocks and bushes. They seem willing to extend their natural growth, for if guided into an evergreen tree, such as Holly or Ilex, they will clamber up to surprising heights. Climbing Aimée Vibert, for instance, which is generally used as a pillar Rose or for some such use as that shown on the opposite page, will rush up high into a tree, as may be seen in the picture (p. 168). The uses of these free Roses are unending, but just now it is their adaptation to house and garden walls that is under consideration. When growing naturally, these Roses throw out young rods of new growth every year ; by degrees the older growths die, and the younger ones, pushing outward, shoot up through the dead and dying branches, both hiding them and displaying their own fresh young beauty.

But on a wall this internal scaffolding of dead wood

cannot be tolerated, and a close watch has to be kept on the plants, and the older growths have to be cut right away at least every two years. How these free Roses will grow over and decorate the porch and walls of a small house of no architectural pretension may be seen from the illustration (p. 182). It is these houses that best lend themselves to the use of the climbing Roses, indeed many that are absolutely ugly, or worse than plainly ugly—debased by fictitious so-called ornament of the worst class—may be re-deemed and even made beautiful by these bountiful and lovely Cluster Roses.

A modest dwelling that has no special beauty or character may by a clever use of climbing Roses be converted into a delightful object. No one could pass the roadside cottage shown in the illustration without a thrill of admiration for the free-growing cluster Rose that covers the walls and wreaths the front of the porch (p. 182).

The little house itself has lost much of its true character from the evident alteration of the windows, which would originally have been either lead lights and casements, or, if sash windows, would have had the panes smaller, with rather thick sash-bars. The large panes destroy the proportion and make the house look too small for them. Some ugly flat frames to all the windows, and pediment-shaped additions to the tops of the lower ones, do much to destroy and vulgarise the effect of what must have been a little building with the modest charm of perfect simplicity. The lead-roofed porch is right, and so is the open

Roses " . . . derived from species of rambling habit that in their native places climb about among rocks and bushes. . . seem willing to extend their natural growth, for if guided. . they will clamber up to surprising heights." Climbing rose Madame Gregoire Staechlin covering the walls and wreathing the windows and porch of a house.

CLUSTER ROSES ON A COTTAGE.

CLUSTER ROSE, BENNETT'S SEEDLING, ON THE PORCH OF MR. MAWLEY'S HOUSE.

wooden railing. One cannot but be thankful that when the windows were altered so much for the worse, the railing was not replaced by a cast-iron "ornamental" atrocity.

When a house is of fine design one hesitates about covering it with flowering plants, but in such cases they find their right places on terrace walls, unless these are decorated with wrought stone balustrading.

The illustration shows an example of good use of the beautiful Garland Rose on the terrace of a good square-built house of middle or late eighteenth century construction. The terrace is not balustraded, and the two or three feet of height gained by the rising of the Rose and the other free growths give the needed sense of security in a kind of living parapet (p. 186).

Many are the Roses for use on garden walls. They are detailed in lists referred to at the end of the chapter on Pillar Roses, and only some of the most remarkable need be here noticed.

In the south of England, walls facing south and south-west are too hot a place for many of the Roses commonly planted against them, although these exposures suit the tender Roses, the Noisettes, Banksias, Macartneys, and Fortune's Yellow, all of rambling growth. Here is also the place for the beautiful Persian Briers, including the scarlet so-called Austrian, the curious Abyssinian *Rosa Ecæ* with yellow blooms the size of a shilling, *Rosa simplicifolia Hardi* with yellow flowers that have a dark blotch at the base of the petal, and *Rosa microphylla*, a flower whose character is quite its own. The double variety has

"Many a beautiful effect may be gained by a Rose planted on one side of a wall and trained to tumble over the top on to the other side. Often a south wall is devoted to rather tender shrubs; in such a place if a hardy cluster Rose. . . is planted on the north side, a good mass of its bloom will come over and help to decorate the walls on the more precious or southern face." Rosa Bantry Bay.

THE GARLAND ROSE ON A TERRACE WALL.

BENNETT'S SEEDLING, THE SAME PLANT AS ON THE PORCH, EXTENDING OVER THE WALL OF BACK YARD.

ALICE GRAY AND FÉLICITÉ-PERPÉTUE ON A VERANDAH.

THE BLUSH BOURSAULT.

ROSES ON A HOUSE WALL THAT WOULD HAVE GIVEN
MORE FLOWER IF THEY HAD BEEN MORE
CLOSELY PRUNED.

CLIMBING AIMÉE VIBERT ; Noisette.

WILLIAM ALLEN RICHARDSON (N.) ON A VERANDAH.

ROSE COMING OVER A WALL.

the best bloom and is very ornamental; in both the double and single the prickly calyx is a remarkable feature, as is also the fruit of the type, which by retaining this curious calyx forms a strange-looking hip.

On garden walls of other exposures in the southern parts of England almost any of the free-growing Roses will do well. Naturally in the colder midlands and in the damper climates of Scotland, Ireland, and Wales the warm aspects may be used for more kinds of Roses, such as the Teas and Hybrid Teas.

Many a beautiful effect may be gained by a Rose planted on one side of a wall and trained to tumble over the top on to the other side. Often a south wall is devoted to rather tender shrubs; in such a place if a hardy cluster Rose, such as Dundee Rambler, is planted on the north side, a good mass of its bloom will come over and help to decorate the walls on the more precious or southern face.

It should be remembered that as Roses on walls want training and pruning that it is well, even if there is an important flower border in front, to have a little blind alley running within a foot or so of the wall. If they are not easy to get at they are apt to be neglected. There must be every facility for training, pruning, mulching and cutting. The pruning in this case consists in the removal of the older wood of these free-growing Roses; it must never be neglected, or the plant will soon grow thin and leggy. Who does not know the starved wall Rose in a worn-out border against a bare wall, with ten or twelve feet of

ROSE FLORA. TRAINED OVER THE TOP OF A WALL.

naked stem and branch and famished growth of flower and leaf covered with green-fly? Perhaps within three feet of its root is a flourishing Ivy, with a stem as thick as a man's wrist, covering half the house and bulging with the loose untidy nests of house sparrows. If we expect a Rose to give its beauty we should at least let it have fair play both above ground and below; in the ground by giving it proper space and nutriment, and above by watching for the time when old wood should be cut out, rampant young stuff tipped, and new flowering wood trained in.

CHAPTER XIII

ROSES FOR CONVERTING UGLINESS TO BEAUTY

No plant is more helpful and accommodating than the Rose in the way of screening ugliness and providing living curtains of flowery drapery for putting over dull or unsightly places. For instance, no object can be much less of an adornment to a garden than the class of ready-made wooden arbour or summer-house "made of well-seasoned deal, and painted three coats complete." Yet by covering it with an outer skin of ramping Roses it may in about three years be made a beautiful thing, instead of an eyesore. The illustration (p. 198) shows a house that has been planted with Crimson Rambler and other free-growing Roses. Larch poles, connected by top rails, have been placed round it. The spreading branches of the Roses will reach out over the rails, and the whole thing will become a house of Roses. Not only will it be beautiful, but the deep masses of leafy and flowery branches will keep off the sun-heat, which, without such a shield, makes these small wooden buildings insufferably hot in summer.

Many an old farmhouse is now being converted into a dwelling-house for another class of resident, and wise are they who consider well before they pull down the old farm buildings. For even a tarred

AN UGLY WOODEN SUMMERHOUSE WITH A PARTLY-GROWN
COVERING OF CRIMSON RAMBLER AND OTHER
FREE ROSES.

BARE OLD FARM BUILDINGS BROUGHT INTO GARDEN USE
BY A PLANTING OF CREEPERS, WITH NEAR BUSHES
OF FREE-GROWING ROSES.

shed, with a thatched or tiled roof, may soon be made beautiful by a planting of these beneficent Rambling Roses. Many of the buildings, shed or barn, cowhouse or stable, may still have the weather-boarding undefiled by gas-tar, and if so, its silvery grey colour is a ground whose becoming quality can hardly be beaten for tender pink and rosy Roses. Dead or unprofitable old orchard trees, too, may have their smaller branches sawn off and be planted with Roses. If they are shaky, some stout oaken props, also rose-clothed, will steady them for many a year. When once these Roses get hold and grow vigorously the amount of their yearly growth is surprising.

Generally among these farm buildings there is, in the enclosed yard, a simple shelter for animals, made of posts supporting a lean-to roof, either against a barn or a high wall. This, without alteration, or merely by knocking through the two ends, may be made into a delightful shaded cloister, each post having its Rose. There would not need to be a climbing Rose to every post, but a climbing and a pillar Rose alternately. The lean-to roof would need some slight trellising, the rougher the better. No material for this is so good as oak, not sawn but split. Split wood lasts much longer than sawn, as it rends in its natural lines of cleavage and leaves fairly smooth edges. Sawing cuts cruelly across and across the fibres, leaving a fringe or ragged pile of torn and jagged fibre which catches and holds the wet and invites surface decay.

"No plant is more helpful and accommodating than the Rose in the way of screening ugliness and providing living curtains of flowery drapery for putting over dull or unsightly places."

DEAD APPLE TREES, ALREADY PARTLY CLOTHED WITH CLIMBING ROSES.

GARDEN ARCH MADE OF DEAD APPLE LIMBS AND CLOTHED WITH IVY AND CLIMBING ROSES.

"*The thought comes that the Rose garden ought to be far more beautiful and interesting than it has ever yet been. In the hope of leading others to do more justice to the lovely plants that are only waiting to be well used, I will describe. . . a Rose garden as I think should be made. In this, as in so much other gardening, it is much to be desired that the formal and free ways should both be used. If the transition is not too abrupt the two are always best when brought into harmonious companionship.*"

These farm places have also commonly old field hedges, some one of which may become the boundary of the new pleasure garden. If it is rightly placed for shelter or for its original purpose of a field fence, or for its newer service, it is better not to grub it up, but to fill its gaps and weak places with free-growing Roses. If it has Thorns, either Blackthorn or Whitethorn, and Hollies, both of some height, it is a chance to be thankful for of showing how these grand rambling Roses will rush up and tumble out, and make lovely dainty wreaths and heavy-swagging garlands of their own wild will. We have only to place them well and show them how to go, to lead and persuade them just at the beginning. In two years' time they will understand what is wanted, and will gladly do it of themselves in many ways of their own—ways much better than any that we could possibly have devised.

Then there is no end to the beautiful ways of making Rose arbours and tunnels, or Rose houses for the children. Dead trees or any rough branching wood can easily be put up and spiked together to make the necessary framework, and the Roses will take to it gladly. An old dead Apple-tree, if it happens to stand where an arbour is wanted, need not even be moved ; another bit of trunk can be put up eight feet away, and the branches of the standing one sawn off, all but those that go the right way. These branches can be worked in to form the top, keeping a stout, slightly curved piece for the front top beam. The Roses seem to delight in such a

DEAD APPLE TREES CLOTHED WITH ROSES OVER AN ORCHARD GATE.

CLIMBING ROSE COVERING AN OLD FARM SHED.

CLIMBING ROSE COVERING A DEAD APPLE TREE.

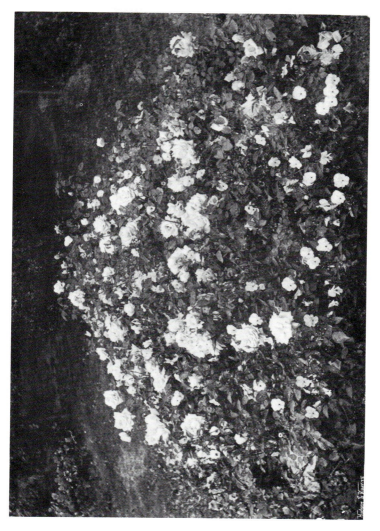

A BED OF TEA ROSE DR. GRILL, (ROSE, SHADED COPPER), ON A CARPET OF TUFTED PANSIES.

rough-built arbour, for they rush up and clothe it with most cheerful willingness.

The back-door region and back-yard of many a small house may be a model of tidy dulness, or it may be a warning example of sordid neglect; but a cataract of Rose bloom will in the one case give added happiness to the well-trained servants of the good housewife, and in the other may redeem the squalor by its gracious presence, and even by its clean, fresh beauty put better thoughts and desires into the minds of slatternly people.

What a splendid exercise it would be if people would only go round their places and look for all the ugly corners, and just think how they might be made beautiful by the use of free-growing Roses. Often there is some bare yard, and it has come within my own experience to say to the owner, "Why not have rambling Roses on these bare walls and arches?" and to have the answer, "But we cannot, because the yard is paved, or perhaps asphalted." Is not a grand Rose worth the trouble of taking up two squares of flagging or cemented surface?

CHAPTER XIV

ROSE GARDENS

ONE of the many ways in which the splendid enthusiasm for good gardening—an enthusiasm which
only grows stronger as time goes on—is showing itself,
is in the general desire to use beautiful Roses more
worthily. We are growing impatient of the usual
Rose garden, generally a sort of target of concentric
rings of beds placed upon turf, often with no special
aim at connected design with the portions of the
garden immediately about it, and filled with plants
without a thought of their colour effect or any other
worthy intention.

Now that there is such good and wonderfully varied
material to be had, it is all the more encouraging
to make Rose gardens more beautiful, not with beds
of Roses alone—many a Rose garden is already too
extensive in its display of mere beds—but to consider
the many different ways in which Roses not only
consent to grow but in which they live most happily
and look their best. Beds we have had, and arches
and bowers, but very little as yet in the whole range
of possible Rose garden beauty.

The Rose garden at its best admits of many more
beauties than these alone. Of the Roses we have
now to choose from some are actual species, and

many of them so nearly related to species that their wild way of growth may well be taken into account and provided for. Thus the beautiful milk-white *Rosa Brunoni* of the Himalayas is at its best climbing into some thin growth of bush or small tree. Many of the numerous new rambling Roses, children of another Himalayan Rose, that have been hybridised with other species, and again crossed to gain variety of colour and shape, willingly lend themselves to the same treatment. Many Roses, even some of those that one thinks of as rather stiff bushes, the Scotch Briers, *Rosa lucida* and the like, only want the opportunity of being planted on some height, as on the upper edge of a retaining wall, to show that they are capable of exhibiting quite unexpected forms of growth and gracefulness, for they will fling themselves down the face of the wall and flower all the better for the greater freedom. The beautiful and fast-growing *Rosa wichuriana*, with its neat white bloom and polished foliage, will grow either up a support or down a steep bank, or festoon the face of a wall far below its roots, and to the adventurously minded amateur disclose whole ranges of delightful possibilities ; while, stimulated by the increased demand, growers are every year producing new hybrids and clever crosses derived from this accommodating plant.

So the thought comes that the Rose garden ought to be far more beautiful and interesting than it has ever yet been. In the hope of leading others to do more justice to the lovely plants that are only waiting to be well used, I will describe and partly

In a Rose garden "there would be the quiet lawn spaces below, whose cool green prepares the eye by natural laws for the more complete enjoyment of the tinting of the flowers whether strong or tender, and. . . cool green woodland carried far upward for the outer framing of the picture. In no other way that I can think of would beautiful groupings of Roses be so enjoyably seen, while the whole thing, if thoroughly well designed and proportioned, would be one complete picture of beauty and delight."

THE USUAL ROSE BEDS ON A LAWN. A KIND OF ROSE GARDEN THAT MAY BE
MUCH IMPROVED UPON.

A NEWLY-MADE ROSE GARDEN (*Rose of three years' growth*).

A NEWLY-MADE ROSE GARDEN (Roses of seven months' growth).

APPROACH TO A ROSE GARDEN FROM WOODED PARK LAND.

FREE-GROWING ROSES AT THE EDGE OF WOODLAND ON THE OUTER EDGE OF A FORMAL ROSE GARDEN.

THE PLANTS AT THE ANGLES OF THE TERRACE PAVING ARE NOT ROSES, BUT THE PICTURE SHOWS WHAT AN EXCELLENT WAY IT WOULD BE OF USING ROSES OF FREE BUSHY GROWTH PLANTED IN SPACES LEFT IN THE PAVEMENT.

A ROSE BORDER ON A STEEP SLOPE. THE GRASS PATH WOULD BE BETTER WIDER.

CLUSTER ROSE HANGING OVER A TERRACE WALL.

illustrate such a Rose garden as I think should be made. In this, as in so much other gardening, it is much to be desired that the formal and free ways should both be used. If the transition is not too abrupt the two are always best when brought into harmonious companionship. The beauty of the grand old gardens of the Italian Renaissance would be shorn of half their impressive dignity and of nearly all their poetry, were they deprived of the encircling forest-like thickets of Arbutus, Evergreen Oak, and other native growths. The English Rose garden that I delight to dream of is also embowered in native woodland, that shall approach it nearly enough to afford a passing shade in some of the sunny hours, though not so closely as to rob the Roses at the root.

My Rose garden follows the declivities of a tiny, shallow valley, or is formed in such a shape. It is approached through a short piece of near home wood-land of dark-foliaged trees, for the most part evergreens; Yew, Holly, and Scotch Fir. The approach may come straight or at a right angle; a straight approach is shown in the plan. As it belongs to a house of classic design and of some importance, it will be treated, as to its midmost spaces, with the wrought stone steps and balustraded terraces, and such other accessories as will agree with those of the house itself.

The bottom of the little valley will be a sward of beautifully kept turf, only broken by broad flights of steps and dwarf walls where the natural descent makes a change of level necessary. The turf is some thirty feet wide; then on either side rises a retaining

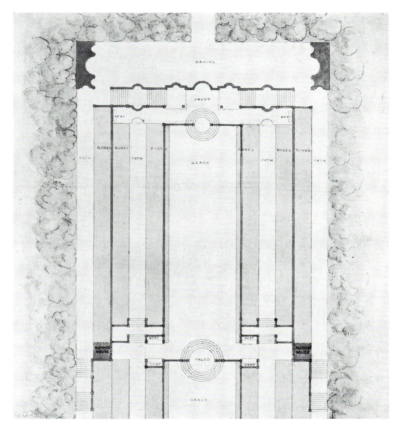

PLAN OF THE UPPER PART OF A FORMAL ROSE GARDEN IN
A SMALL VALLEY WITH WOODLAND ABOVE.

RAMBLING ROSE RUNNING INTO TREES IN THE WOOD
EDGE, *AS DESCRIBED, BOUNDING THE FORMAL
ROSE GARDEN.*

wall crowned by a balustrade. At the foot of this, on the further side, is a terrace whose whole width is about twenty-four feet. Then another and higher retaining wall rises to nearly the level of the wooded land above. This has no parapet or balustrade. The top edge of the wall is protected by bushy and free-growing Roses, and a walk runs parallel with it, bounded by rambling Roses on both sides. On the wooded side many of the Roses run up into the trees, while below Sweet-brier makes scented brakes and tangles.

The lawn level has a narrow border at the foot of the wall where on the sunnier side are Roses that are somewhat tender and not very large in growth. On the terraces there are Roses again, both on the side of the balustrade and on that of the retaining wall. The balustrade is not covered up or smothered with flowery growths, but here and there a Rose from above comes foaming up over its edge and falls over, folding it in a glorious mantle of flower and foliage. It is well where this occurs that the same Rose should be planted below and a little farther along, so that at one point the two join hands and grow together.

So there would be the quiet lawn spaces below, whose cool green prepares the eye by natural laws for the more complete enjoyment of the tinting of the flowers whether strong or tender, and there is the same cool green woodland carried far upward for the outer framing of the picture. In no other way that I can think of would beautiful groupings of Roses be so enjoyably seen, while the whole thing, if thoroughly well designed and proportioned, would be one complete picture of beauty and delight.

In a place that binds the designer to a greater degree of formality the upper terrace might be more rigidly treated, and the woodland, formed of Yew or Cypress, more symmetrically placed. On the other hand there is nothing to prevent the whole scheme being simplified and worked out roughly, with un-dressed stones for the steps and dry walling for the retaining walls, so as to be in keeping with the other portions of the grounds of any modest dwelling.

If a Rose garden is to be made on a level space where any artificial alteration of the ground is inex-pedient, it will be found a great enhancement to the beauty of the Roses and to the whole effect of the garden if it is so planned that dark shrubs and trees bound it on all sides. The plan shows a simple scheme where this is arranged. A central space of turf has Rose borders in the form shown. Outside is a wide grass walk, and beyond that dark shrubs. On the four sides grassy ways pass into the garden ; while the whole outer edge of the Rose beds is set with posts connected by chains on which are pillar and free-growing cluster Roses placed alternately.

At each outer and inner angle of the design will be a free-growing Ayrshire or one of the now nume-rous Rambler group. Each of these will furnish the length of chain on its right and left, while Pillar Roses will clothe the posts between.

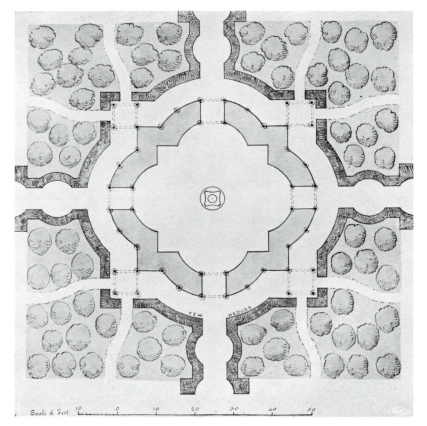

Scale of Feet   10   0   10   20   30   40   50

PLAN OF A ROSE GARDEN ON LEVEL GROUND ENCLOSED BY
YEW HEDGES, BEYOND WHICH ARE TALL EVER-
GREENS, SUCH AS ILEX OR CYPRESS.

RAMBLING ROSE (Double Arvensis), RUNNING INTO TREES AT WOOD EDGE, as described at p. 225.

*VISCOUNTESS FOLKESTONE (H.T.), A BEAUTIFUL ROSE
FOR MASSING IN BEDS.*

FREE ROSES GROWN AS GARLANDS.

A ROSE GARDEN IN THE MAKING; SHOWING FRAMEWORK OF POLES AND LATHS.

"*Many Roses... show that they are capable of exhibiting quite unexpected forms of growth and gracefulness, for they will fling themselves down the face of [a] wall and flower all the better for the greater freedom.*"

The background of dark trees is so important that I venture to dwell upon it with some degree of persistence. Any one who has seen an Ayrshire Rose running wild into a Yew will recognise the value of the dark foliage as a ground for the tender blush white of the Rose ; and so it is with the Rose garden as a whole.

The wisdom of this treatment is well known in all other kinds of gardening, but with the tender colourings of so many Roses it has a special value. It should be remembered that a Rose garden can never be called gorgeous ; the term is quite unfitting. Even in high Rose tide, when fullest of bloom, what is most clearly felt is the lovable charm of Rose beauty, whether of the whole scene, or of some delightful detail or incident or even individual bloom.

The gorgeousness of brilliant bloom, fitly arranged, is for other plants and other portions of the garden ; here we do not want the mind disturbed or distracted from the beauty and delightfulness of the Rose. From many of the Rose gardens of the usual unsatisfactory type other kinds of gardening are seen, or perhaps a distant view, or a carriage road, or there is some one or other distracting influence that robs the Roses of the full exercise of their charm. Even in a walled space, unless this is darkly wooded round, it is better not to have Roses on the walls themselves, but rather to have the walls clothed with dark greenery.

The beneficent effect of neighbouring dark trees

may be seen in the picture of the Rose arches (p. 237). Trees of dark or dusty foliage serve well as Rose backgrounds, whether of the greyish tone of the common Juniper or the richer greens of Thuya or Cypress, Yew or Holly.

In the few instances that can be given in a book it is impossible to consider a hundredth part of the many varying circumstances of different gardens. Each place has its own character, and the choice of site for the Rose garden will necessarily be governed by the natural conditions of the place.

One illustration (p. 220) shows a Rose border made just under a terrace wall. The ground to the right slopes too sharply to allow of a broader grass walk without having another retaining wall below ; had it not been for this, a space of turf as wide again, between the border and the Rose hedge, would have been better. Here also is plainly seen the value of the dark evergreen trees above (p. 220).

A ROSE GARDEN AMONG CYPRESSES.

RAMBLING ROSE THE GARLAND, GROWING INTO TREES,

IRON ARCHES IN A RECTORY GARDEN WITH ROSE SIR JOSEPH PAXTON.

TEA ROSES OF THE DIJON CLASS.

CHAPTER XV

ROSES AS CUT FLOWERS

THERE is scarcely any Rose that we can wish to have in our gardens that is not also delightful in the cut state. A china bowl filled with well-grown Hybrid Perpetuals, grand of colour and sweetly scented, is a room decoration that can hardly be beaten both for beauty and for the pleasure it gives, whether in a sitting-room or on the breakfast table. The only weak point about cut Roses is that their life is short. The day they are cut they are at their best, the next day they will do, but the third day they lose colour, scent, and texture. Still it is so delightful to any one who lives a fairly simple life in the country to go out and cut a bunch of Roses, that the need for their often renewal is only an impulse towards the fulfilment of a household duty of that pleasant class that is all delight and no drudgery.

Tea Roses last quite a day longer than Hybrid Perpetuals, but they need more careful arrangement, for many of them have rather weak stalks and hang their heads. Still these may be avoided and only strong-stalked ones used. In most cases they are best by themselves, without the addition of any other flowers. In my own practice the only notable exception I make to this general rule is with the

239

Cabbage and Moss Roses, the Damasks, and other old garden kinds. Whether it is that they are so closely associated with what one considers the true old garden flowers, or for some reason of their own ordaining, I could not say, but about midsummer I have great pleasure in putting together Cabbage, Moss, and Damask Roses with Honeysuckle and white Pinks, and China Roses also with white Pinks. The combination of these few flowers, all of sweetest scent, seems to convey, both by sight and smell, the true sentiment of the old English garden of the best and simplest kind.

Large Roses are top-heavy, and every one who is used to arranging flowers, must at some time or other have been vexed by a bunch of Roses carefully placed in a bowl conspiring together to fling themselves out of it all round at the same moment. It is well worth while to have wire frames made for the bowls that are generally in use. Two discs of wire netting with a top rim and three legs of stouter wire can be made by any whitesmith or ironmonger or by the ingenious amateur at home. The lower tier of netting should be an inch from the bottom of the bowl, to catch the lower end of the stalk. I have often used three garden pots, one inside another in a china bowl, thus making three concentric rings and one centre for stalk space. Stiff greenery, like Box or Holly, kept low in the bowl out of sight, also makes a good foundation.

Roses are best also with their own leaves, the chief exception to this being the beauty of red-tinted summer shoots of Oak, which in July and August are

A COTTAGE NOSEGAY OF GARDEN ROSES. DUNDEE RAMBLER, ROSA ALBA, MAIDEN'S BLUSH, AND CABBAGE ROSE,

CLIMBING ROSE MADAME ALFRED CARRIERE (H.N.), ONE OF THE EARLIEST AND
LATEST TO BLOOM.

DOUBLE WHITE SCOTCH BRIER; THE WILD BURNET ROSE, ITS ANCESTOR, LYING ON THE TABLE.

A BOWL OF LATE SEPTEMBER ROSES.

BURNET ROSE AND SCOTCH BRIERS.

A BOWL OF TEA ROSES WITH BERBERIS LEAVES.

ROSE D'AMOUR, THE DOUBLE FORM OF R. LUCIDA, PINK, WITH DEEPER CENTRE.

One-third life size.

ROSA ALBA; DOUBLE AND HALF-DOUBLE.

A GLASS OF COMMON PINK CHINA ROSE.

OCTOBER ROSES AND CLEMATIS PANICULATA.

CHINA ROSES AND IVY IN MID-OCTOBER.

DUNDEE RAMBLER (Ayrshire), ARRANGED FOR STANDING HIGH, SO AS TO BE SEEN RATHER FROM BELOW.

extremely harmonious with the colourings of the Teas and hybrid Chinas. Also in the autumn I like to use with my Roses some sprays of the wild Traveller's Joy (*Clematis vitalba*).

Some of the free-growing Roses are beautiful cut quite long, even to a length of three to four feet. They are delightful decorations in rooms of fair size, arranged in some large deep jar that will hold plenty of water, not only for their sustenance, but as a weighty counterpoise to the flower - laden branches that will hang abroad rather far from the centre of gravity. Roses like Madame Alfred Carrière, that flower in loose bunches on long stems, and the crimson half - double Reine Olga de Wurtemberg, with its incomparable foliage that can be cut almost any length, show by their natural way of growth how they must be arranged in long branching ways. The Ramblers and Ayrshires, too, are beautiful cut in yard-long branches, but are difficult to arrange. Special ways have to be devised for overcoming their desire to swing round flower-side down. But placed high, on the shoulder of some cabinet about six feet from the ground, with the lovely clusters trending downward, they are charming and beautiful room ornaments.

Great care should be given to assorting the colours and in putting together kinds that have some affinity of blood and harmony of tint. It is well never to mix Hybrid Perpetuals and Teas, except, perhaps, some of the more solid Teas of the Dijon class. But Roses well assorted are like a company of sympathetic friends—they better one another.

It is always well to have two or three of the same range of colouring, with perhaps one harmonious departure, such as Madame Lambard, Papa Gontier, and Laurette Messimy, or G. Nabonnand, Vicountess Folkestone, and Hon. Edith Gifford, or Souvenir de Catherine Guillot, White Maman Cochet, and Anna Ollivier.

The same suggestion will be found of use in arranging them in beds, for a jarring mixture, such as one of the orange-copper Hybrid Teas, with kinds of cool pink and white, will have an unsatisfactory effect. Both may be lovely things, but they should not be placed together. But to learn to observe this—first of all to see that it makes a difference, then to become aware that it might be better, and finally to be distinctly vexed with an inharmonious combination, these are all stages in growth of perception that should be gone through in the training of the Rose enthusiast's mind and eye.

It is best and easiest to learn to do this with the cut flowers, and a pleasant task it is to have a quantity of mixed cut Roses and to lay them together in beautiful harmonies—best, perhaps, in some cool, shady place upon the grass—and then to observe what two or three, or three or four kinds, go best together, and to note it for further planting or indoor arrangement. Then, as an example of what is unsuitable, try a Captain Christy and a Madame Eugène Résal together, and see how two beautiful Roses can hurt each other by incompatibility of kind and colour.

ROBERT DUNCAN (H.-P.)

SOUVENIR DE LA MALMAISON (*Bourbon*), AND CLIMBING
AIMÉE VIBERT (*Noisette*), IN MID-SEPTEMBER.

LADY EMILY PEEL (an old blush-white garden Rose), IN SEPTEMBER.

CLIMBING ROSES ON THE BALCONY OF AN ITALIAN VILLA.

CHAPTER XVI

ROSES IN ENGLISH GARDENS ON THE RIVIERA

IT is very surprising to find how few kinds of Roses are grown in gardens on this coast, and consequently a mere list is rather disappointing, the fact being that it is the beauty and the abundance of their flowers that constitutes the charm rather than the very great variety of kinds. The cause is very easy to comprehend. Those who care for their gardens do not as a rule come out much before Christmas, and leave at the latest by the middle of May, so that any Rose that does not flower freely during the late autumn or early spring is of little importance, however beautiful it may be. Moreover, the great sun power and the fatal Rose beetles that tear the petals to ribbons in May prevent the latest Roses being of real value, while the gorgeous blaze of Geraniums, Gazanias, Petunias, and such summer flowers destroys the tender tones of those Roses which bloom late.

It is the climbing Roses that are the joy of the gardener here. They grow rampantly and flower profusely, whether they be grown trained to walls, pergolas, arches, pillars, and such like, or if they simply are planted near a tree, preferably an Olive or Cypress, and fling their sprays of blossom down from the very highest to the lowest branches, with never a pruning knife or gardener's shears to mar their native grace.

The Banksian Roses must have the first place for beauty and abundance, though only the big white R. B. Fortunei is fairly perpetual, and decks its glossy evergreen foliage with isolated flowers through the whole winter. The single yellow Banksian Rose, introduced not more than twenty years ago from Italy, and first admired in Sir Thomas Hanbury's well-known garden at La Mortola, deserves a special notice, because it is fully three weeks earlier than the double forms in spring, and gives a delightful summer effect in the month of March in sunny situations, and is even more rampant and floriferous than any other member of the family, becoming a real tree itself.

There are two forms of the double yellow Banksian Rose. For richness of colour and beauty of flowering spray I think Jaune decidedly the best, and indeed, for its period of flower, the most effective of all. The second and less well known form—that I know as Jaune serin — has larger, paler flowers on longer stems, is decidedly less brilliant in effect, but has just the same delicate perfume the small double white exhales, and which is curiously enough denied by many people who are appreciative of other scents.

The common double white Banksian Rose is the most abundant and ubiquitous of all, and is as much the ornament of trees, walls, pergolas, and pillars in the month of April and early May as the common Ivy is in more northern climates. It is everywhere,

BANKSIAN ROSE CLIMBING INTO OLIVE AND CYPRESS.

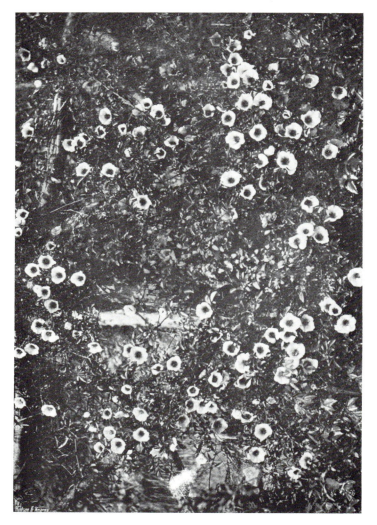

ROSA SINICA or CAMELLIA

and nowhere out of place, though it loses its leaves in the month of January.

Rosa sinica, commonly called Rose Camellia on this coast (another eastern Rose), is an especial favourite here. Rampant in growth, abundant in its single white flowers, which first open in March, with thorny shoots whose red stems and glossy foliage enhances the purity of the petals, it heralds the arrival of spring, and prefers light and poor soils where many other Roses fail. Its new companion and hybrid, R. S. Anemone, promises to become even more beautiful, and being of a soft rose-du-Barri tint, will soon find its way everywhere, as there is no climbing Rose of its particular and lovely shade of colour.

Rosa bracteata.—The Macartney Rose is rarely seen, as it flowers so late in spring, but as it blossoms well in autumn when *R. sinica* is barren, it should not be omitted. Its glossy, perfectly evergreen foliage is quite unique, and the long sprays tipped with its scented flowers in November are greatly admired.

R. Marie Leonidas (a double form of this Rose) is the freest winter bloomer of this section. Most beautiful in a few gardens, it is not grown as much as it deserves, as it is not a flower for the market, which alone is the criterion of worth to French gardeners. It should not be omitted by the amateur.

R. Fortunei.—To China again we are indebted for this lovely climber, perhaps in a sense the most notable of those yet mentioned, for it does not and cannot show its real beauty in northern gardens, where it needs shelter. Plant it near an Olive or

Cypress, and in three or four years it will entirely cover the tree with a mantle of delicate sprays. Its flowers, lovely in shades of apricot and rose, contrast brilliantly with its apple-green and slender foliage. It is only a spring bloomer, but none the less indispensable on account of its grace and beauty.

R. Cloth of Gold or Chromatella.—A grand Rose, so rarely seen now that it should not be forgotten. Its individual blooms are unsurpassed in size and colour by any yellow Rose, and its December flowers are most beautiful of all when in a rich soil and sheltered position. The fact that its lovely buds bruise so easily, and that it is a special prey to mildew, are the reasons why it is now only to be found in a few gardens where it is extra happy. This is one of the Roses for which this coast was famous until the advent of Maréchal Niel entirely displaced it.

R. Maréchal Niel.—"Good wine needs no bush" is specially applicable to this grandest of all yellow climbing Roses, for it advertises itself everywhere in every garden, and by autumn pruning produces even lovelier flowers in December than can be seen in May when grown on sunny terraces. For Rose arches and arcades it is indispensable, and contributes largely to the effect of luxuriant beauty. What a pity its flowers do not hold up their heads as *R. Chromatella* does.

R. Lamarque, with its lemon-centred and lemon-scented heads of flower, is the finest double white climbing Rose yet raised, although it dates from sixty years ago, and is still fresh, young, and beautiful. It blooms so well in late autumn and again in early

Gertrude Jekyll often wrote how important it was that the individual should reflect himself in his garden: "for the very essence of good gardening is the taking of thought and trouble. No one can do good decorative work who does it merely from a written recipe. The use of such a book as this is to describe enough to set the Rose pilgrim on his road."

LAMARQUE (N.), WHITE, SHADED LEMON, FLOWERS NATURALLY IN CLUSTERS.

April, that it is found in every garden, and we who come out from England have a special admiration for its masses of white flower, because it refuses to show its real beauty out of doors in England, and grows too rampantly when under glass.

Old Roses are, you will see, all my theme, so I feel no compunction in saying that the old Rose, Gloire des Rosomanes, semi-double though it be, is the only perfectly perpetual winter-blooming climbing red Rose yet raised. It is the only old Rose that is never flowerless throughout the severest weather on this coast, and it is particularly brilliant and fragrant both in autumn and in spring when the Banksian Roses need a rich red to contrast with their white and golden-buff tones. It is well known to many folk as the Bordighera Rose, though I do not know it is more abundant there than elsewhere. One of its seedlings, General Jacqueminot, is a household word, known and grown everywhere, and there are two more of its seedlings worth mention—Bardou Job, which has merit, though it is not a winter bloomer, and also the new Noella Nabonnand, which is a decided advance in size and beauty, and is said to be a really good winter-blooming deep red Rose, a desideratum in these parts.

We all know the brilliant little China Rose Cramoisi Supérieur, but somehow I never saw in English gardens a good specimen of its variety or seedling Cramoisi Grimpant, and this latter is next in importance among climbing red Roses, for it will climb to fully twenty feet high, and cover itself with its rich crimson flowers all the winter through if only there be no frost. For hedges and pillars this is most decorative when it contrasts with the Banksian or Lamarque Roses, and forms a splendidly toned background to all light-coloured Roses.

Another climbing red Rose that I have never seen to advantage in England is heavily weighted by its senseless name, La France de 1889. Nevertheless, it is a very large, fragrant, and deep rose-red flower of great beauty, which makes prodigious shoots in autumn, and flowers by degrees, beginning at the top in December and continuing to do so lower down the long shoots throughout the season. It is of the very largest size, fragrant, and double, but I think it is capricious in some gardens, as beauties are apt to be.

A Rose much seen I only mention to reprobate in this climate, that is, Reine Olga de Wurtemberg, which though so good in England is here so fleeting and ugly in colour that I regret to see it, even though it be only for one week in early spring. Not so Marie Lavallée, a delightful blush pink, semi-double climbing Rose, the latest and the earliest of its colour, vigorous and fresh in every way.

Duchesse de Nemours is a fragrant and bright pink climber, double, and of fine size and form, which is only to be found in a few old gardens, but is far too good a Rose to pass by. In December, and again in May, it will produce a wonderful effect. It seems less easy to propagate from cuttings than other Roses, and is to be found in only one nurseryman's list, but I am glad to say its merit has been recognised, and a stock of it will, I believe, soon again be obtainable. To my fancy it is far preferable to the deeper coloured Reine Marie Henriette, so very common all along the Riviera, and which in December, mingling with Rêve d'Or, has a great charm, even if it be not the very best of all.

R. La Grifferaie, which we seem only to know as a stock for other Roses, is a very brilliant and luxuriant climber in late spring, intensely bright pink in its clusters. The growth and foliage of this Rose are prodigious, and it requires a large space to do itself justice ; were it perpetual it would rank as one of the best. Waltham Climber No. 3 shows to great advantage on this coast. Its long strong shoots are clothed with its scarlet-crimson flowers early in spring, and give a fair sprinkling of blooms continuously during winter when grown on a sunny pergola.

No mention has been made of Gloire de Dijon and its many seedlings, for they do not show to as great advantage as in more northern gardens.

Belle Lyonnaise is fairly good, but there is one of more modern date, Duchesse d'Auerstadt, which proves the exception to the rule, and is most excellent in every way. From its growth it is evidently from Rêve d'Or on one side, and is quite the finest, freest, and best of all golden-yellow Tea Roses of climbing habit. It will no doubt entirely displace Rêve d'Or, being its superior in every way, and this, to those who know that old Rose on this coast, is saying much.

Noisette Roses.—After Lamarque, which has already received its due notice, Jaune Desprez must be mentioned on account of its perfume and beauty in spring. Curiously enough it is not always a winter bloomer, but it still luxuriantly adorns many an old garden.

Idéal is essentially a Rose for this coast. In spring it even rivals Fortune's Yellow, but it comes in several weeks later and is deeper in its rosy tones. Did it but bloom at all in winter it would be unsurpassable.

Dr. Rouges is the most intensely brilliant shade of orange-red that I know, and when fully proved will be invaluable as a climber when its winter blooming is established. The rich claret-red shoots in January are almost as brilliant as any flower could be.

William A. Richardson no longer climbs here, but flowers splendidly in winter as a straggling bush.

Pink Rover must certainly not be omitted from the list of climbing Roses, for there are so few of its fresh and lovely shade of colour. It is very sweet-scented, blooms abundantly before Christmas, and wherever grown is at once a favourite. It seems to revel in the conditions here.

Grüss an Teplitz, a seedling between Cramoisi Grimpant and Gloire des Rosomanes, is another very delightful semi-climbing Rose on this coast. Most brilliant red in colour, sweet-scented and free, it has hardly yet been sufficiently planted, so its merits are not fully established.

Hybrid Teas are decidedly the most in vogue now, owing not only to their size and beauty, but to the length of stalk with which they may be cut. As garden Roses they are equally valuable. Caroline

Testout entirely takes the place of La France, which never showed itself to perfection on this coast. Marquise Litta has made its mark also, and is very rich and bright in colour during the winter. Gloire Lyonnaise and Captain Christy are splendid winter bloomers, but the flowers are not considered so valuable for the market. Belle Siebrecht is also becoming a very popular Rose, while Mme. Jules Grolez is considered worthless, for its petals are soft and easily spoilt, and it does not grow with anything like the same vigour. There is no doubt that many of the Roses that do well in English gardens do not enjoy a more southern climate, and it is curious to remark how the descriptions of French raisers refer generally to Roses grown in a hotter climate than England, so that their descriptions are not so likely to mislead in the south as those in the north are apt to imagine.

Hybrid Perpetual Roses are little grown, and are chiefly used for late autumn cutting out of doors. For the first three months of the year they are now flowered under glass, so that they can be cut with the long stems required in France. I need only mention Paul Neyron (so fine in December), Ulrich Brunner, Baroness Rothschild, Mrs. John Laing, General Jacqueminot, and Eclair as the best and most useful here. The growth of Roses under glass for market in January, February, and early March has become a great industry, and is largely displacing the hardy winter-blooming Teas grown on the sunny terraces.

Tea Roses, which not only bear but enjoy the summer heat and drought, flowering freely in November and December after the autumn rains and pruning, are cultivated not only in gardens, but as a field crop, and the December crop of bloom is the most valuable, so that everything yields to that. To name any but the most valuable is unnecessary here, and, roughly speaking, Nabonnand's catalogue of his own seedlings represents what has been most grown during the last twenty years. Of these, however, many are obsolete.

Isabelle Nabonnand is one of the few really good winter Roses I have never seen grown in England. One of the oldest, it still is worth growing in any garden. Its blush-centred white blooms are fairly double, and yet open freely through the winter.

General Schablikine has at last found its way to England. For many years this was the only rose-coloured Tea to be depended on in winter. Now that glass is so much used, and larger and longer stalked blooms are required, it is only used as a decorative garden Rose. Marie Van Houtte is another old Rose that is gradually being superseded, as its flowers obstinately refuse to hold up their heads, but its beauty and freedom make it indispensable in the winter garden. Paul Nabonnand has for some years reigned supreme from the beauty and freedom of its pale pink blooms in December. It is *the* Rose that with Schablikine produces the most summer-like effect during the winter. Fiametta Nabonnand is a very good flesh-white Rose, as indeed are all

those that are named after the Nabonnand family,
particularly for winter blooming. Papa Gontier, so
bold in growth, so rich in petal, is the most useful
of all winter Roses for cut bloom. Its size and
brilliant rose-pink colour are remarkable in this
climate. I have never seen it in its true character
in England. The fields and hedges of Safrano, the
first of all winter-blooming Roses, deserve a passing
mention, though now, save as a hedge Rose, it is
not worth a place. Its abundance of flowers about
Christmastide is its chief attraction, and at that season
it is still sent in quantity to northern cities.

Antoine Rivoire is the Rose that has made a mark
lately, both in the garden and in the grower's ground.
Its beauty and fresh pink and white colouring (white
in December), and its fine vigorous stems crowned
with bold upright flowers, have at once raised it to
high favour. It looks as if it were a cross between
Captain Christy and some old Tea like Rubens, and
is better than either. Mme. Cadeau Ramey is a
very sweet and lovely garden Rose, but has not as
yet at all the same vogue, being of the Devoniensis
type.

The China Roses and Hybrid Chinas do not find
favour here, they are too fleeting and too thin, and
Tea Roses give us more beauty. For instance, Beauté
Inconstante, a Tea, has not only even more brilliant
orange-scarlet tones than any hybrid China, but
it is so free and hardy, as well as solid in petal,
that it puts to shame its cousins that are so welcome
in northern gardens.

THE DOUBLE YELLOW BANKSIAN ROSE.

MADAME FALCOT (T.), DEEP APRICOT, DERIVED FROM SAFRANO.

HYBRID TEA ROSE ANTOINE RIVOIRE; *BLUSH AND YELLOW*
TINTING, ROSE CENTRE, 4 *inches.*

Cramoisi Supérieur is lovely as a dwarf hedge, but is not nearly so good a winter bloomer as the climbing form Cramoisi Grimpant ; so it is in hedgerows and avenues that the glowing masses of this are seen in company with the pale pink *Indica Major*, which here takes the place of the Hawthorn hedge.

PART II

PLANTING, PRUNING, AND PROPAGATING
ROSES; EXHIBITING, GROWING UNDER
GLASS, ETC.

By EDWARD MAWLEY

A STANDARD JULES MARGOTTIN (H.P.)

CHAPTER XVII

PLANTING ROSES

To hasty or otherwise improper planting may be more often traced the unsatisfactory condition of Roses in gardens large or small than to all other causes put together. The term " planting " as here used is a comprehensive one, as it is intended to include the choice of the position of the Rose garden, the preparation of the beds, as well as the actual planting of the Roses themselves. This question, then, of planting, is one of supreme importance.

Position.—The best site for Roses is an open yet sheltered one, though as little shut in by trees or buildings as may be. On the other hand it must not be too much exposed, for although Roses delight in a free atmosphere they have a great objection to be frequently swept by high winds. Shelter from the north and east is most necessary, but exposure to strong winds from almost any quarter is undesirable. Bearing these facts in mind, the position best complying with them should be chosen, and, if necessary, a high hedge or belt of trees be planted on the side where shelter is most needed. Care must however be taken that this hedge, or tree belt, is sufficiently distant from the Roses to prevent the possibility of its roots finding their way at some future time into the Rose beds. One of the best hedges for the purpose may be formed of the common Arbor-vitæ, as it is of tolerably quick growth, makes an excellent screen, and its roots extend but a short distance on each side. Wherever it is possible Roses should be allowed a separate bed or beds to themselves, and not be planted with other flowers. Where it is intended to grow a large number of Rose plants, beds might with advantage be made in the virgin soil of some paddock or other piece of pasture land, such as may frequently be found adjoining country gardens.

Soil.—A deep, strong loam is the very best soil for Roses—land on which an exceptionally good crop of wheat could be grown. But as this ideal soil for a Rose garden is seldom to be found ready to hand, an endeavour must be made to supply the existing soil with those ingredients and physical qualities in which it is most deficient. For instance, should it be a stiff clay, it must, if necessary, be drained. If not so retentive as to require draining, a liberal quantity of burnt earth and long stable manure, sand, &c., must be incorporated with it. If on the other hand the existing soil be too light and porous, some heavier loam should be mixed with it, and cow instead of stable manure introduced. If on examination the soil be found not only porous but also shallow, some of the chalk, gravel, or sand beneath must be entirely removed and replaced by the heaviest soil, not absolute clay, obtainable in the neighbourhood.

The Preparation of a Rose Bed.—When the preparation of the bed is completed it should contain suitable and well-enriched soil to the depth of at least two feet. Roses prefer a somewhat stiff soil, and yet not one so retentive as to prevent any superfluous moisture from passing readily away from the neighbourhood of their roots. In a soil which is too light the plants are unable to avail themselves as they should of the nourishment brought down to their roots by rain or artificial watering. Such soils moreover become unduly heated in hot and dry weather—whereas, above everything, Roses delight in a consistently cool root-run. Soils which quickly feel the changes of temperature above ground from cold to heat and heat to cold cannot be regarded as suitable for Roses.

In the case of a moderately good Rose soil the beds should be thus prepared. The earth from one end of the bed should be removed to the depth of a foot, and three feet wide, and wheeled to some spot close to the other end of it. Having taken out this trench, the bed should then be bastard-trenched throughout to the depth of two feet ; that is to say, it should be dug over, but none of the lower soil brought to the surface. When performing this operation a liberal quantity of manure—farmyard manure for preference —should be incorporated with the soil, filling in the last trench with the earth which had been previously wheeled there. This will make a Rose bed sufficiently good for all ordinary purposes. Should, however, the bed be required for Roses intended to produce exhibition blooms, it will be well to loosen the soil with a fork at the bottom of each trench, and on

this loosened soil to place, grass downwards, the top spit of an old pasture. Then in addition to the farm-yard manure some half-inch bones should be mixed evenly with the soil as the trenching proceeds, together with some turfy loam, for there is nothing which will so greatly improve almost any soil for Roses as a liberal supply of fibrous loam. If possible the beds should be completed in August or September, so that the soil in them may have some chance of settling down before the Rose plants are ready for removal to their new quarters in November.

Staking out the Beds.—As soon as the preparation of the bed is completed it will be well to make a rough plan of it on paper and indicate upon it the position that each Rose is intended to occupy. This can readily be done by arranging that the dwarf plants be two feet and the standards three feet apart. These distances will answer admirably for plants intended for the production of exhibition blooms ; but for Roses for ordinary garden or home decoration the distances between the plants might with advantage be increased to two feet six inches for dwarfs and to three feet six inches for standards. In the case of varieties described in the catalogues as "very vigorous," and which are intended to be grown as bushes, the plants must be five or even six feet apart.

The Treatment of Rose Plants when received from the Nurseries.—When unpacking Roses, care should be taken that neither the roots nor the branches are injured, and on no account should the roots be allowed to become in any way dry. As soon as

"Roses are so comparatively modest, they are so accommodating and so little fastidious, that with very moderate preparation and encouragement they can be made to succeed. . . Then it is but few that aspire to the honours of the show table, while nearly every one who is master of a rood of land now desires to enjoy it as a garden." Rosa Ballerina in a cottage garden.

R. MACRANTHA. A NATURAL HYBRID OF CANINA AND GALLICA.

separated, the plants should be "heeled in"; that is to say, a shallow trench should be made in the kitchen garden or other convenient spot, and the roots of the new Rose plants be placed in it, and afterwards watered and completely covered with soil. When heeling the plants in, it will be advisable to place them in the trench in the order in which they are to be afterwards arranged in the beds, so that the required varieties may be readily removed from the trench as they are wanted without disturbing the rest. If the weather be frosty at the time the plants arrive, it will be well not to unpack them at all, but to leave them in their straw bundles until the weather changes and they can be properly heeled in. If for any reason the package be unduly delayed in transit and the bark on the shoots presents a shrivelled appearance, a deeper trench should be dug, and the plants, branches and all, placed lengthways in it and completely buried. When removed from the trench in three days' time the shoots will be found to have recovered their freshness.

The Actual Planting.—This can be undertaken at any time between the beginning of November and the end of March, but the best time of all is early in November. Should the ground be sodden or frozen when the Roses arrive, the planting must be deferred until in the one case the superfluous moisture has passed into the subsoil, and in the other until the frost is quite out of the ground. In order to prevent the exposure of the roots to sunshine or drying winds it will be a good plan to take only a few plants at a time from the place where they have been heeled in and to place a mat over them when brought to the side of the bed. A square hole for each plant should be made, not more than six inches deep and sufficiently large to hold the roots when spread out horizontally. A plant should then be taken from beneath the matting and placed in the hole, taking care to spread out the roots evenly all round. Some fine soil, free from manure, should next be worked with the hand between the roots and above them to the depth of three inches, and afterwards trodden down with moderate firmness, so as not to bruise the roots. After adding more soil, that in the hole should again be pressed down, more firmly this time, and a final treading given when the hole is filled up. Firm planting is of the greatest importance to the after welfare of the plants. In planting Roses intended for exhibition, or where extra attention can be given them, it will be well to place a little leaf-mould at the bottom of each hole, and to work in, among and above the roots, a few inches of the same material instead of the fine soil. Failing leaf-mould, some finely chopped fibrous loam may be used ; if of a somewhat gritty nature so much the better. In each case a small handful of bone-dust should be sprinkled over the layer of leaf-mould or fibrous loam. The principal advantage of these additions is that they enable the plants to become more quickly established, and also allow of the planting being proceeded with, when, owing to the wet nature of the soil in the beds, it would not be otherwise practicable. No manure should be allowed to come in contact with the roots themselves at the

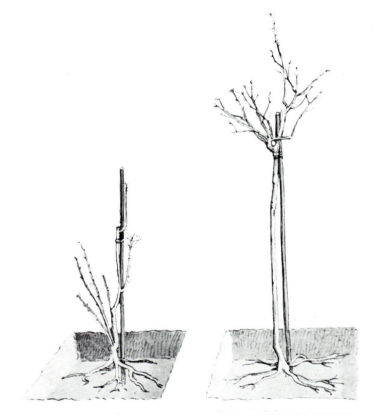

METHOD OF PLANTING DWARF AND STANDARD ROSES.

time of planting. The roots when they become active will soon find out the manure and appreciate it, but in a dormant state it is more like poison than food to them.

Planting Climbing or Pillar Roses.—These strong growing varieties are often treated as if they could take care of themselves and therefore required less care in planting than other Roses, whereas the contrary is the case. The hole made to receive them should be two feet six inches square and two feet deep. The existing soil, if fairly good, should be enriched with a liberal addition of farmyard manure, and the planting proceeded with as described in the previous paragraph. If the natural soil, however, be poor and thin some of this should be removed altogether and better soil substituted. The reason why these extra vigorous Roses require a larger quantity of good soil is because the roots have to support a much larger plant, and as a rule they are intended to occupy the same position for a great number of years.

Staking and Labelling.—All standard Roses should be firmly staked as soon as planted, or better still, the stake should be driven into the centre of the hole made to receive the Rose before the latter is planted. The upper part of the climbing Roses should be also fastened either to the support up which they are intended to be trained or to a temporary stake at the time of planting. Ordinary dwarf Roses will not require staking if planted firmly as directed, and if any extra long shoots they may have are shortened.

All Roses as soon as planted should be labelled.
Permanent metal labels may be obtained already
stamped with the name of almost any Rose of
Mr. J. Pinches, 3 Crown Buildings, Crown Street,
Camberwell, S.E.

CHAPTER XVIII

PRUNING ROSES

THERE are few things connected with Rose culture so little understood by amateurs and gardeners generally as pruning ; and it must be acknowledged that the number of different kinds of Roses, and the very different treatment many of them require at the hands of the pruner, cannot but make this operation seem at first sight a very puzzling one. The following simple directions will, however, serve to show that it is not nearly so complicated as it is generally thought to be.

Mr. W. F. Cooling, in an excellent paper read before the National Rose Society in 1898, very cleverly separates the numerous classes of Roses into two broad and distinct divisions. In the first of these divisions he places the Hybrid Perpetuals, Hybrid Teas, and Teas—all of which (the climbing varieties alone excepted) require more or less hard pruning ; while in the second division we find the Hybrid Sweet-briers, the Austrian Briers, all the extra vigorous and climbing Roses and many garden or decorative Roses, which, although of comparatively dwarf habit, need little spring pruning, or none at all.

Before proceeding to treat of the various kinds of Roses more in detail it may be well to point out

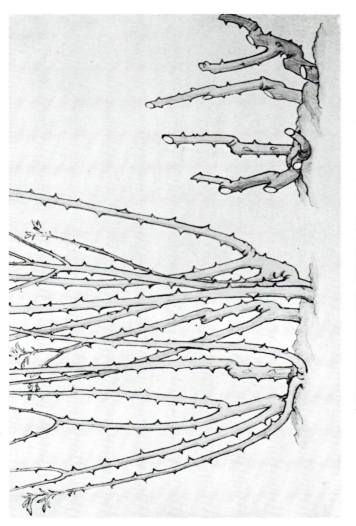

AN EXHIBITION ROSE BEFORE AND AFTER PRUNING.

a few considerations which apply to the art of pruning generally. In the first place, the object of pruning is to add increased vigour to the plant, and at the same time to regulate its growth. It is difficult to understand at first, but nevertheless perfectly true, that the more severely a Rose plant is pruned the stronger will be the shoots which result from that apparently murderous treatment. There is also another general rule which naturally arises out of the foregoing, and that is the weaker the plant the more closely it should be cut back, and the more vigorous it is the longer should the shoots be left. As a matter of fact, pruning consists of two operations which are altogether distinct. Firstly, thinning out all the decayed, crowded and otherwise useless shoots; secondly, the pruning proper, that is to say, the shortening back of the shoots that remain after the thinning-out process has been completed. There is no Rose that does not from time to time require some thinning out, but there are many which require very little, if any, shortening back. When removing the useless shoots they should be cut clean out, either down to the base of the plant or to the shoot from which they spring, as the case may be. Then again, in the case of dwarf or bush Roses, the pruner has to decide whether he requires a small number of extra large flowers or a larger number of moderate-sized ones. If the former, both the thinning out and pruning must be severe, whereas in the other case rather more shoots should be allowed to remain, and these may be left longer. After a very cold winter the pruner will find that, except in the case of quite hardy varieties, he has little choice in the matter of pruning, the keen knife of the frost having come before him and already pruned his Roses after its own ruthless fashion. In this case all the dead shoots should be cut away, and those that remain be afterwards examined. At first sight they may appear altogether uninjured, but on cutting them it will be seen that scarcely any sound wood is anywhere to be found. The best test of frost injuries is the colour of the pith. If this be white, cream-coloured, or even slightly stained, the wood may be regarded as sufficiently sound to cut back to, but if the pith be brown sounder wood must be sought for, even if this be only met with beneath the surface of the beds.

Armed with a pruning knife, which should be of medium size and kept always with a keen edge, an easy pair of gardening gloves, a hone on which to sharpen the knife, and a kneeling pad, the pruner will require nothing more except a small saw, which will prove of great service in removing extra large shoots and dead stumps. A really good secateur may be used instead of a knife if preferred. In pruning, the cut should be always made almost immediately above a dormant bud pointing outwards. In all but an exhibitor's garden the best time to prune Roses is early in April.

1. **Roses which require to be more or less closely pruned.**—Under this heading is included at least three-fourths of the Roses most frequently grown

in gardens at the present time as dwarf plants. All the weak and moderate - growing varieties must be pruned hard each year, and also all plants, with few exceptions, intended for the production of extra large flowers. But those Roses which have been planted for the decoration of the garden, or for the production of cut flowers, need not be so severely dealt with, while those planted as Rose bushes will require comparatively light pruning.

Hybrid Perpetuals.—The first year after planting all the dead, sappy and weakly shoots should be cut clean out, and those remaining left from three to six inches in length, whatever the variety may be. This hard pruning is necessary the first spring, but in the following years it need not be so severe. The dead, sappy, weakly and worn-out shoots should, as before, be cut clean out, also some of the older ones and any others where they are too crowded, more particularly those in the centre of the plant. The object kept in view should be an even distribution of the shoots allowed to remain over the entire plant, except in the centre, which should be kept fairly open to admit light and air. In pruning, the shoots may be left from three inches to one foot in length, according to the condition of the wood, the strength of the plant, and the object for which the blooms are required. Provided that the frosts of the previous winter months will allow, that the plants are sufficiently strong, and that the shoots are not permitted to become in any way crowded, the upper shoots may be as much as three feet above the ground. In

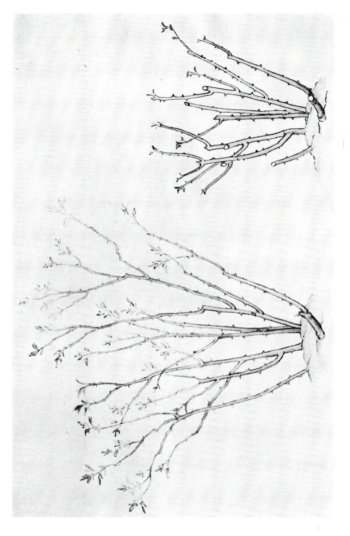

A GARDEN ROSE BEFORE AND AFTER PRUNING.

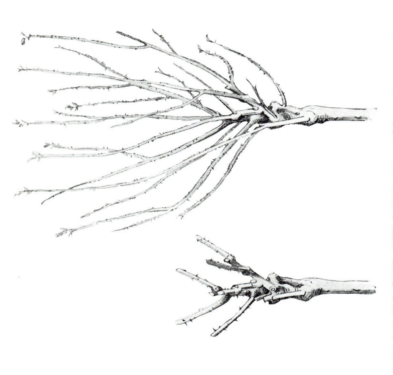

A STANDARD H.P. ROSE; THE SAME ROSE PRUNED AND UNPRUNED

this way good-sized bushes may in a few years be obtained, which will form handsome objects in the garden and yield a large number of good flowers. By similar treatment the more vigorous varieties in this and other sections may be induced to become pillar Roses, or even to climb some distance up a wall. It is the want of hardiness in many of the Roses of the present day, that are usually grown as dwarf plants, which alone stands in the way of their suitability for the formation of handsome bushes or for their employment as climbers and pillar Roses.

Hybrid Teas.—The pruning of the Hybrid Teas should be carried out on similar lines to those recommended for the Hybrid Perpetuals, only it should be less severe. Indeed, in the case of varieties like La France, which are of sufficiently strong growth to allow of this being done, better results are obtained by moderate thinning out, and rather light pruning, as is recommended in the case of the Hybrid Perpetuals, where good-sized bushes are required.

Teas and Noisettes.—Owing to the tender character of their shoots, it is only after a mild winter that the pruner has much choice in the method of pruning. In any case, all the decayed, weak, and sappy shoots should be cut clean out, and where there are enough sound shoots left they should be shortened back one-half their length.

Bourbons.—The Bourbons should be pruned in the same way as advised for the strong-growing varieties of the Hybrid Perpetuals and Hybrid Teas.

Provence, Moss, and China. — These hardy Roses should be well thinned out, to prevent their growths becoming crowded, and the remaining shoots shortened one-half their length.

2. Roses which require very little pruning.—To whatever section a Rose may belong, if it be grown as a climber, or as an arch or pillar, it will not do to cut it back hard, or it will bear but few if any flowers. But there are also certain other Roses which, although not of extra strong growth, will not flower satisfactorily if cut back at all severely. It is by cutting away the flowering wood of such kinds that the greatest mistakes in pruning usually occur.

Climbing, Pillar, and other strong-growing Roses.— In the spring these need very little attention beyond securing the best shoots in the positions they are required to occupy, and to shorten back or remove altogether any other shoots which may not be required at all. Within July, however, all these strong-growing Roses should be examined, and every year some of the shoots which have flowered be entirely removed and the best of the strong young growths encouraged to take their place, cutting out altogether those not needed. The object of thinning out the shoots that have flowered, and tying or laying in the strong young shoots of the current year, is to enable the latter to make better growth, and by exposure to light and air to become ripened before the winter sets in.

Austrian Briers.—Beyond removing the dead, in-

One of the features of Gertrude Jekyll's "planned" rose garden included roses "foaming up . . in a glorious mantle of flower and foliage." The modern shrub rose Nevada.

LADY MARY FITZWILLIAM (H.T.), ROSY FLESH COLOUR.

jured, and worn-out shoots, the Austrian Briers should not be touched at all with the knife.

Scotch Briers.—These require similar treatment to the Austrian Briers.

Hybrid Sweet-briers.—The Sweet-briers need no spring pruning at all; but in July, after flowering, it will be well to cut out some of the older shoots where crowded, in order to give the younger ones a chance of making better growth.

Pompon.—The free-flowering miniature Pompon Roses should have their shoots well thinned out, and those left shortened one-half their length.

Rugosa or Japanese Roses.—This hardy section requires but little pruning. Some of the old and crowded shoots should be entirely removed, and the younger growths either tied in or moderately shortened.

Banksia.—The pruning of this particular class of Rose differs somewhat from that of nearly all the climbers in that they require but little thinning. After flowering, the strong shoots of the present year's growth not required to furnish the plant should be removed, and the rest of them tied in and slightly shortened. Care should be taken not to cut away the twiggy growths, as the flowers are borne on these laterals.

Gallica or French Roses.—Only the striped varieties in this class are now grown. They should be pruned in the same way as recommended for the Provence Roses.

Single-flowered Roses.—As these belong to so many

different sections, it is impossible to give the exact treatment all of them require. Those of vigorous growth should be pruned as advised for other Climbing and Pillar Roses, while the bush and dwarf varieties should be only thinned out, and the points of the remaining shoots removed. The few dwarf Hybrid Perpetuals bearing single flowers should, however, be rather severely pruned.

Pegging down Roses.—When suitable varieties are selected, this way of growing Roses in beds has much to commend itself; indeed, in no other way can such a number of blooms of the larger-flowered Roses like the Hybrid Perpetuals be obtained from the same number of plants. In the spring only a few of the longest and best shoots on each plant should be retained. After cutting off just the ends of these long shoots they should be carefully bent and pegged down to within a few inches of the soil. In the following spring the shoots that have flowered should be cut away, and the strong young growths pegged down in their place.

JEAN PERNET (T.), LEMON YELLOW.

WHITE BARONESS (H.P.)

CATHERINE MERMET (T.); LIGHT ROSY FLESH COLOUR.

CHAPTER XIX

PROPAGATION OF ROSES

THERE are several other ways of propagating Roses, but the one most frequently employed and the most satisfactory is by budding.

Dwarf Stocks.—Many people imagine that all the dwarf or bush Roses they see in gardens are growing on their own roots, whereas in ninety-nine cases out of a hundred the roots of the plants are those of some Brier stock. The three stocks most in favour at the present time are the Brier-cutting, the seedling Brier, and the Manetti.

The only difference between the Brier-cutting and seedling Brier is that the former is obtained by making cuttings of the ordinary hedgerow Brier, while the latter is the result of sowing the seed of that Brier. They are both excellent stocks, and there are scarcely any Roses which will not unite with and grow well on either of them. The roots of the Brier-cutting are thrown out more horizontally than those of the seedling Brier, and are therefore more accessible to light and air and to any liquid or other surface nourishment that may be given them. On the other hand the downward tendency of the numerous roots of the seedling Brier enables the Roses budded on it to withstand drought better, and it is if anything the more permanent stock of the two. The Manetti stock answers well in some parts of the country, such as the northern districts of England, and on certain soils, but cannot be so generally recommended as the other two stocks that have been mentioned. In most cases the roots of the Manetti, which is a foreign Brier, gradually decay, and the Rose budded on it, after a time, either dies outright or is kept alive by the roots thrown out round the collar of the plant by the Rose itself. It has another great defect in that the foliage of the Manetti is not easily distinguishable from that of many cultivated Roses, so that the suckers from this stock often pass unnoticed. Indeed one seldom goes into any ordinary garden without meeting with these suckers. In many cases the Rose has entirely disappeared, and the shoots of the stock alone remain.

It is not necessary to explain the method of raising any of these dwarf stocks, as all three can be obtained early in the autumn at a cheap rate from any Rose nurseryman. As soon as they arrive they should be planted one foot apart and three feet between the rows. For the convenience of budding they should be planted only about four inches deep and afterwards earthed up like potatoes as far as the main stem extends.

Standard Stocks.—The only stock used for standards, half-standards, and dwarf standards is the hedgerow Brier. These may be purchased during November from a nursery, or any local labourer used to such work will obtain as many as required from the wild

Briers in the district. These stocks should be trimmed of any side shoots, cut to the length wanted, and planted two feet apart and four feet between the rows. The root should be cut away to within, say, two inches of the stem and not be left like a hockey-stick. The best stocks are those of the second year's growth.

Budding Standard Stocks.—Budding is one of those things which cannot readily be learnt from printed instructions, but which any proficient in the art will be able to teach the beginner in a few lessons, and which a little practice afterwards will soon render quite easy to him. A few hints may, however, be useful when the mechanical process has been mastered. For instance, in budding standard stocks a single rather long slit is preferable to the somewhat shorter T-shaped one usually employed, as the transverse cut weakens the shoot of the Brier and often causes it to snap off in high winds where it has been made. It is also a good plan to give the roots of the stocks a good drenching with water before they are budded, as it will cause the bark to come away from the wood more readily than it otherwise would have done. Budding can be done at any time during the summer ; the early part of July is usually the best period of the year to begin, as the majority of the shoots are then in that half-ripened condition which is so desirable—that is to say, neither too sappy nor on the other hand too old and dry. The shoots of the Rose from which the buds are taken should be in the same half-ripened condition, and the buds themselves only

VISCOUNTESS FOLKESTONE (H.T.); CREAMY WHITE,
SHADED FLESH COLOUR.

moderately plump and consequently quite dormant. If the bark does not come away readily from any shoot when the handle of the budding knife is inserted, it is useless to try and bud on it. When the prickles on either the shoot of the Brier to be budded or on the shoot of the Rose from which the bud is to be taken come off easily and there are at the same time fresh green leaves at the end of that shoot, it is certain to be in the best condition possible for budding. The Hybrid Perpetuals and Hybrid Teas will be found easier to bud than the Teas. The buds should be tied in moderately firmly but not too tightly. In a fortnight's time they may be tied afresh, this time more loosely. After budding, none of the budded shoots of the Brier should be touched with the knife until November, when the longest and most vigorous may be shortened about one-third of their length.

Budding Dwarf Stocks.—The stocks should be kept well earthed up until budding time, when the surrounding soil should be removed with a small hand fork from a few of the Briers as they are wanted. The main stem should then be cleaned with a rag and the slit made in it for the insertion of the bud. The T-shaped slit, previously objected to in the case of standard stocks, may here be made, and a single bud (or if preferred two buds close together) be inserted in it. The buds should be inserted quite low down in the stem near the roots and not in the upper part of it. The instructions given when treating of budding standard stocks as regards watering, the time of year, the selecting of the buds, and also as to tying and retying them after insertion, apply equally to those dwarf stocks.

Raising Rose Plants from Cuttings.—Now that excellent Rose plants can be obtained ready made, as it were, from the nurseries at such reasonable prices, it seems hardly worth while trying to raise them from cuttings, besides which, budding is a much more certain and quicker method of increasing a stock of Roses. To ensure the greatest measure of success the following directions may be followed with confidence, as they are the outcome of the experience of one of the most skilful raisers of own-root Roses that we have ever had. A cucumber or other cold frame should be placed on hard ground and filled with a mixture of loam, sand and leaf-mould in nearly equal proportions to the depth of six inches. This compost should be made very firm and afterwards well watered. In a few days it will be ready to receive the cuttings. The best time to commence operations is towards the end of September. The cuttings should be taken from shoots which have borne the first crop of Roses of the year, as they will then be in the half-ripened condition required. They should not be cut from the plant but stripped off with a slight heel. The cuttings should be about four inches in length and thus prepared. All the leaves should be cut off except the two lower leaflets of the two upper leaves. They must be dibbled in and made very firm at the base or they will not strike. The cuttings should be inserted six inches apart and three inches deep, leaving the remaining inch with its leaflets to peep out above the compost. After the cuttings have been planted they should for a time be kept close, admitting a little air to prevent the leaflets damping off. In severe weather the frame must be covered with sufficient matting or other material to keep out frost, or the cuttings will be lifted by its action on the compost and so prevented from rooting. Early in May in the following year they should be taken up with a ball and potted, kept close for a time in a frame, and then gradually exposed to the air and sunshine. In August they will be ready to plant out. The Roses which best answer to this treatment are the stronger growing varieties, for the moderate growers, if they succeed at all, take a long time before they make good plants.

Rose cuttings may be struck in the open ground under a north wall or other shady spot, planting them in sandy soil as above advised; but owing to the disturbing influence of frost and other causes the percentage of successes will not be nearly so great as when they are afforded the protection of frames.

Grafting.—This method of propagation is scarcely ever employed by amateurs, and it is therefore unnecessary to describe it here. It is used by nurserymen, principally for raising pot Roses and as a rapid way of increasing the stock of any new or rare variety.

CHAPTER XX

THE ENEMIES OF THE ROSE

THERE is scarcely any other plant which is attacked by so many or such persistent enemies as the Rose. Strange to say, writers on Rose culture, in enumerating these, invariably omit to mention the most potent enemy of all, and that is, adverse weather. It is not only that these adverse weather conditions often inflict more serious and lasting injuries than all the other enemies of the Rose put together, but they are also indirectly responsible for the worst attacks from insect and other pests. Taking all classes of Roses together, there is perhaps no climate in the world so favourable to their perfect development as that of the British Isles, and, provided seasonable weather could always be depended upon, these islands would be a perfect paradise for the rosarian. Unfortunately this is far from being the case, as more or less unseasonable weather must be regarded in this country as the rule rather than the exception, and consequently he is kept in a continual state of anxiety as to what unfavourable climatic changes his favourites may next be called upon to encounter. No doubt one reason for these anxieties is due to the fact that most of our cultivated Roses are only half-hardy plants, and

315

therefore peculiarly susceptible to all kinds of un-favourable weather influences.

Frosts.—These may be divided into two classes—the winter frosts and the spring frosts. Against the former the protection provided cannot well be too complete, whereas very moderate means will mostly be sufficient to ward off injuries from spring frosts; and yet against the ill effects of these spring frosts there is practically no remedy, unless it be syringeing or spraying the frosted foliage with water very early in the morning in order to thaw it before sunrise. For at that season it is not so much the damage done by the frost itself that has to be guarded against as the sudden thawing of the frozen leaves by the sun shining on them. Of course the reason why spring frosts are so difficult to deal with as compared with winter frosts is that in the one case the plants are clothed with delicate young foliage, whereas in the winter it is only necessary to protect the lower portion of the leafless shoots.

Early in December all the dwarf or bush Roses, whether Hybrid Perpetuals, Hybrid Teas, Teas or Noisettes, &c., should have the surrounding soil in the beds drawn over the centre or crown of the plants to the height of several inches. In other words, they should be earthed up like potatoes. This earthing up is generally confined to the Teas, but no amateur will regret having given his other dwarf Roses this extra attention should the winter prove unusually severe, for there are comparatively few varieties which will be found at pruning time

ROSEBANK METHOD OF PROTECTING STANDARD TEAS.

after such a winter with perfectly sound wood even within a few inches of the surface of the beds.

Standard Roses are less easily protected. Bracken, cut in September before it has become brittle, should be secured to the heads ; or a more effectual protection may be afforded the standard Teas by first drawing the shoots of the plant together and then lightly thatching the head with straw or bracken fastened above it to a firm stake, with one or more ties lower down, as may be necessary to prevent the straw or bracken from being blown aside in high winds. Tender wall Roses, such as Maréchal Niel, are best protected by fastening over them some fine cotton netting, or by placing bracken, small sprigs of fir, or other light evergreens, among the branches.

Drought.—In dry weather it will be well to give all the plants a good watering (at least half a gallon to each Rose) once a week, either with clear water or weak liquid manure. On the following day the beds should be hoed to keep a loose surface, which will be of the greatest help in preventing the soil beneath from becoming quickly dry again. Another plan is to give each plant a thorough watering with clear water and then to cover over the surface of the beds with a mulching or covering of half-decayed manure. The objection to a mulching, which should never be applied before June, is that many consider it unsightly, and the birds are sure to scratch among it and so scatter the manure over the grass or other paths between the beds.

Insect Pests.—Against the foregoing and other ad-

verse weather influences the Rose grower is to a great
extent powerless, whereas insect pests, if attacked
with promptness and perseverance, can, as a rule,
be readily subdued. The great thing is to watch for
their appearance and at once proceed to destroy the
first comers, and when this is done to continue to
harass the enemy until the attack has entirely ceased.
It is, as a rule, only when any insect pest has been
allowed to obtain a firm footing that there need be
any difficulty in getting rid of it. Good culture is a
great help, as well-nourished and healthy plants do
not suffer so much from insect and other attacks as
those that are ill-fed and weakly. The only remedy
against all the larger insects that attack the Rose,
like caterpillars, grubs, beetles, sawflies, &c., is hand-
picking; whereas the smaller ones, like greenfly,
thrips, red spider, &c., may be best kept in check
by syringeing. Where Roses are largely grown, a
knapsack spraying-pump will be found very useful in
distributing and spraying insecticides and fungicides.

Grubs and Caterpillars.—The Rose maggot and several other equally destructive leaf-rolling grubs and
caterpillars are generally the first pests to attack the
Rose in the spring. They will be found curled up
in the young foliage, and must be sought for every
few days and crushed between the thumb and finger,
or much damage will be done. This is not a pleasant occupation, but unfortunately there is no other
remedy except it be to pinch off the affected leaves
and afterwards burn them or throw them into a
strong solution of salt and water.

The next enemy to appear will be the frog-hopper or cuckoo-spit, a little pale green or pale yellow frog-like insect which will be found hidden in the centre of a small patch of froth deposited either in the axils of the leaves or on the leaves themselves. This, again, must be hunted out and destroyed by means of the thumb and finger, or removed with a small brush and deposited in the salt and water solution before mentioned.

The Boring Grub.—Holes will be often noticed in the tops of the stems of standard Roses ; these are made by this pith-boring grub. As a preventive the ends of standard Roses should be painted with " knotting " at planting time, and the same precaution should be adopted with the standard stocks. If the holes have been already made, a piece of copper wire thrust sharply down them will destroy the grubs ; a little putty is used to close the holes afterwards. The same grubs also occasionally pierce the shoots of Roses, and seem especially fond of those made by standard Brier stocks. In this case, as soon as observed, the hollow ends of the shoots should be squeezed until firm wood is met with, and then cut off. In this way the boring grub will be crushed and the affected part of the shoot removed.

The Rose Aphis or Greenfly.—In some seasons these tiny creatures are very numerous and troublesome, and if not frequently destroyed increase very rapidly. Most exhibitors keep greenfly under entirely by the skilful use of the thumb and finger. This only shows how easily such pests may be kept in check,

"For spaces between garden and wild, for sloping banks, for broken ground. . .for all sorts of odds and ends of unclassified places about the home grounds, the rambling and free-growing Roses seem to be offered us by a specially benevolent horticultural providence."

if attacked directly they make their appearance and never afterwards allowed to congregate in any great numbers. Occasional sharp syringeing with a garden-engine with clean water will be found in most cases sufficient. Should this, however, prove ineffectual, the following well-known remedy may be used instead. Take two ounces of quassia chips and boil them in a gallon of water, adding a tablespoonful of soft soap before the mixture becomes cold. Or one of the many insecticides in the market may be tried, keeping strictly to the directions supplied with the bottle.

Thrips.—These tiny creatures often injure Rose blooms in hot and dry weather, especially those of the Teas, by giving the petals a brown and bruised appearance. Spraying or syringeing with clean water is the best remedy to employ, even at the risk of spoiling some of the existing blooms.

Red Spider.—This is another dry-weather enemy, and so small as not to be detected with the unaided eye. It generally attacks the lower sides of the leaves, and if not kept in check causes them to fall from the plant prematurely. The same remedy as for thrips is advisable. Crimson Rambler, when grown in hot or confined positions, is rather subject to this pest. In dealing with large plants like this, it will be found a good plan to use a small watering-pot with a fine rose, and each evening in dry weather to wet both sides of the leaves by swinging it sharply up and down and across the climber.

Fungoid pests—Mildew.—Of all the insect and fungoid

enemies of the Rose this is, as a rule, the most trouble-some to deal with. It appears as a white mould on the foliage, and if not promptly dealt with will quickly spread from one plant to another over the whole collection. It occurs at all seasons, but principally in autumn, when, if not checked, it will prevent the plants from flowering as freely as they otherwise would. Flowers of sulphur is a sure preventive, but each attack must be dealt with on its first appearance, and the application repeated until a cure is effected. A very simple way of applying the sulphur is by shaking it lightly over the affected plants by means of a fine muslin bag the first calm evening after the mildew is detected. Although only the upper surface of the leaves are dusted over it will be found in practice that the action of the sun will vaporise the sulphur and cause the surrounding atmosphere to be impregnated with it. Syringeing or spraying with the following liquid will also prove effectual, more especially if the under side of the leaves can be wetted with it. To make this mixture half an ounce of potassium sulphide should be dissolved in a gallon of hot water, which should be well stirred as the sulphide of potassium dissolves; when cold the liquid will be ready for use. Warm days followed by cold nights are the most frequent causes of this pest, also a close, muggy atmosphere.

Red Rust or Orange Fungus.—This is much more variable than mildew, and in many gardens is seldom if ever seen, while in others, particularly those on hot and dry soils, it is frequently very destructive to the foliage in the autumn. On its first appearance a few sulphur-coloured spots will be noticed either on the leaves or shoots. In the next stage it increases and becomes a bright orange, ultimately turning black. There is no practical remedy for this fungus, as unlike mildew it vegetates inside instead of on the surface of the foliage.

CHAPTER XXI

EXHIBITING ROSES

IT is often said by those who are beginning Rose culture that they have no idea of ever exhibiting their flowers, but that they simply intend to grow Roses for their own pleasure and for the decoration of their garden. However, after a few years, if their enthusiasm has not by that time altogether evaporated, the care and attention they have given their plants has led to such excellent results that they are often tempted to enter the lists, in order to test their skill against that of other competitors. The great charm that the Rose possesses over most other flowers for exhibition purposes is that it is a true amateur's flower —a flower that any amateur with moderate leisure can cultivate entirely with his own hands ; or if the collection be too large to allow of this being done, he can undertake the lighter and more important parts of the work himself and leave the digging, manuring and watering to be carried out by the gardener under his own special supervision.

The directions that have previously been given as to planting, pruning, &c., apply, for the most part, to exhibitors and non-exhibitors alike. The principal difference consists in the more constant care and attention that the exhibitor is obliged to give his plants in order to keep himself in line with other competitors. It may be well, however, to draw attention to those details of culture which require special care on the part of the exhibitor.

In order to obtain exceptionally fine blooms his collection must be kept clean and well nourished, and at the same time the strength of each plant must be directed into certain restricted channels; in other words, the object should be to have strong and healthy plants, bearing only a limited number of shoots.

Planting.—The Roses may be grown in separate parallel beds five feet wide, containing three rows of plants, with grass paths between the beds. More frequently, however, a piece of ground, either in part of the garden itself or in an adjoining field, is dug up and prepared to receive the whole collection. In the latter case the Roses should be arranged in double lines; that is to say, between each second row of plants a space three feet wide should be left to enable the cultivator to attend readily to the wants of the Roses on each side of this space or pathway. The plants in the rows should be two feet apart, and the same distance should separate the rows. By this arrangement much time is saved, a matter of great importance, considering that each plant will require to be visited if not every day at all events every other day during the growing and exhibiting seasons. It is a mistake to grow a larger number of plants than can receive this amount of individual attention.

Pruning.—The best month in which to prune the

EXHIBITION ROSES IN MR. MAWLEY'S GARDEN AT ROSEBANK.

ERNEST METZ (T.); SALMON, TINTED ROSE

Hybrid Perpetuals and Hybrid Teas is March. It will be well to commence operations early in that month, and to continue the work at intervals during the course of it. When thinning out the shoots of the Hybrid Perpetuals, from three to six shoots, according to the strength of the individual plant, should be allowed to remain. By the best shoots is meant those which are the strongest and at the same time well ripened ; gross, sappy shoots are of little service. When pruned the shoots should be left from three to six inches in length, according to the vigour of the variety—the stronger growers being the least severely pruned.

The Hybrid Teas will also require close pruning as a rule, but the shoots of the strong-growing varieties should be left longer than is recommended for the Hybrid Perpetuals.

The pruning of the Teas must be deferred until April, when, after thinning out the weak, sappy and dead shoots, those that remain should be cut back half their length. Of course, should the previous winter have been unusually severe there will be little choice in the matter, for in that case, after removing the dead wood, the shoots which remain will have to be cut back until sound wood is met with, even should this be beneath the level of the soil.

Insects and other Pests.—These must be diligently sought for and prompt measures taken to destroy them and thus prevent them from spreading. For this purpose a daily inspection of the plants during the growing season will be necessary. It cannot be too often repeated that most of these pests can with comparative ease be kept in check if dealt with directly they make their appearance, but when once they have become established, the difficulties of the cultivator are increased tenfold.

Thinning out the Young Shoots.—As the object of the exhibitor is to allow each plant only a limited number of shoots and to confine the flow of sap to these particular growths, it will be necessary soon after the young shoots appear to remove nearly all the other growths until the first crop of flowers has been produced. It is not advisable to begin this thinning-out process too early, as, in the case of harm from spring frosts, some of the later-made shoots may be required to take the place of some of those originally designed for the production of the exhibition blooms ; besides which, it is only when the young shoots are moderately advanced that it will be possible to judge which of them it will be advisable to retain or to remove. According to the strength of the plant, from three to six flowering shoots should ultimately be left on each. This art of thinning out is an important one and can only be mastered after some little experience. As a rule the growths that are likely to bear the best flowers are the strong ones which come from the top bud of the shoots that have been pruned. Some of the moderately strong shoots which spring from the base of the plant may also be retained, but not so the extra strong sucker-like growths. These should be cut down to within six inches of the ground, for not only will they monopolise an undue proportion of the

HON. EDITH GIFFORD (H.T.)

TWO TEA ROSES. ERNEST METZ (in basket), MADAME DE WATTEVILLE (in glass).

vigour of the plant, but the blooms they produce will be found as a rule to be coarse and unfit for exhibition. This process of thinning should be continued until the buds on the selected shoots are showing colour.

Manuring.—As Roses are gross feeders, it will be necessary to keep the plants well nourished by the threefold application of (1) farmyard or other animal manure, (2) artificial manure, and (3) liquid manure.

(1) In the autumn a good dressing of half-rotten manure—farmyard for preference—should be lightly dug into the beds between the plants, taking care to disturb the roots as little as possible.

(2) In March, and again in May, either Clay's fertilizer, or other artificial Rose manure, should be dusted around each plant, and afterwards mixed with the surface soil by means of a hand-fork. A small handful of either of these manures will be a sufficient application for each Rose.

(3) As soon as the flower-buds are formed the plants should be watered once a week with liquid manure. The first watering, especially if the soil be at all dry at the time, should be very weak. The strength of the liquid after this may be increased, but at no time should the colour be deeper than that of pale ale. An excellent liquid manure may be made by mixing in a tubful of water some fresh cow manure, soot, and guano, in the following proportions: three parts cow manure, one part soot, and one part guano. After these ingredients have been thoroughly mixed with the water, the concen-

trated liquid thus obtained should be freely diluted with clear water before being used. The day after each watering the surface soil should be hoed or lightly forked over to keep it open and accessible to light and air. It is often thought by non-exhibitors that the fine blooms they see at the Rose shows are almost entirely the result of heavy manuring. This is a great mistake, for the size and quality of the flowers depends much more on the free use of the hoe and the unremitting attention that exhibitors bestow on their plants than on the amount of nourishment they may have received in the way of manure.

Mulching.—On hot, dry, shallow soils, it will be necessary to cover the ground on which the Roses are growing with a layer of half-decayed manure in order to keep it moister and less liable to changes of temperature than it would otherwise be. This mulching should, however, not be put on earlier than the beginning of June. Mulching should be dispensed with wherever it is not absolutely needed, as a frequent loosening of the surface soil is no doubt preferable to any such covering.

Disbudding.—At the end of each shoot that has been left on the plants after they have been thinned will ultimately appear, as a rule, three flower-buds. Of these only the centre one should be allowed to remain, the two others being removed as soon as this can conveniently be done. Some use a pointed quill for this purpose, but with a little practice these small buds can be easily taken off with the fingers.

MRS. PAUL (*Bourbon*), PINK.

ROSEBANK SHELTER FOR EXHIBITION ROSES.

Shading.—The blooms of some varieties, and more particularly the crimson Hybrid Perpetuals, are very liable to become burnt if exposed to the direct rays of the sun in hot weather. It will therefore be necessary to afford them some protection. There are many kinds of shades used for this purpose, but the simplest and most efficient are those made of calico stretched tightly over a conical frame made of stout zinc wire, as they are cool, well-ventilated, and sufficiently waterproof, and yet do not seriously obstruct the light. These shades should be 12 inches across in the widest part, and 9 inches high. The zinc socket attached to the frame must be made to slide up and down a square wooden rod in which holes have been pierced at intervals, so that by means of a metal pin the shade can be adjusted to any height required. These zinc frames can be made by any blacksmith, or a smaller shade of the same kind can be obtained ready made of Mr. J. Pinches, of Crown Street, Camberwell. It is advisable to have a good supply of these shades, as they not only shield choice blooms from the sun, but are still more useful in protecting them from rain and heavy dews.

Rose Boxes.—These are usually made of half-inch deal, and are painted throughout dark green. The following are the regulation sizes: viz., for twenty-four blooms, 3 feet 6 inches long ; for eighteen blooms, 2 feet 9 inches long ; for twelve blooms, 2 feet long ; for nine blooms, 1 foot 6 inches long ; and for six blooms, 1 foot long. For eight trebles (three blooms arranged in the box triangularly), 3 feet

6 inches long; for six trebles, 2 feet 9 inches long; and for four trebles, 2 feet long. All the boxes must be 4 inches high in front and 18 inches wide. These are all outside measurements. Inside each box there should be a tray pierced with holes to receive the tubes in which the blooms are exhibited.

Exhibition Tubes. — The best form of exhibition tube is that known as Foster's Tube, as the bloom can be placed by means of the wires supplied with the tubes at any required height without raising the tube itself, and there is a holder in front for the reception of the card on which the name of the Rose is printed or written. These tubes can be obtained of Mr. H. Foster, Ashford, Kent.

Cutting the Blooms.—If the show be a local one and easy of access it will be well to cut the most forward blooms on the evening of the day previous to the exhibition, and those less advanced and likely to improve on the plants during the night, early on the following morning. But if the show be at a distance it will be advisable to cut the blooms early in the evening, as it is found that if cut when they are going to sleep, as it were, in the evening, they develop less rapidly on the journey to the show, and consequently travel better than those cut in the morning when they are growing rapidly. It is no use cutting any blooms which are fully expanded, except in rare cases, as they will be too far advanced for exhibition by the time they reach the show. The choicest half-developed blooms should be selected; that is to say, those which are large for the variety,

HYBRID TEA ROSE MADAME JULES GROLEZ, ROSE PINK, 4 *inches.*

TEA ROSE, MADAME CHARLES, FLESH, WITH ORANGE
AND ROSE TO CENTRE; 4 *inches.*

and at the same time regular in shape and of good colour. The boxes should in the first instance be placed in a cool shed, the tubes filled with water, and the surface of the box covered with the freshest and greenest moss obtainable. It is not a good plan to set up Roses in a shady place in the open air. This being done, the selected blooms, as they are cut, should be placed in the tubes and labelled. The blooms must be cut with stems sufficiently long to allow of their ends reaching the water when raised to the required height at the exhibition. A little experience will show in what stage of development the different varieties, according to their respective staying power, require to be cut. The best blooms should next be chosen, and after having been wired, should be placed in the box intended for exhibition and labelled. Blank labels of a suitable size can be obtained of Messrs. Blake and Mackenzie, School Lane, Liverpool, or they can be had from the same firm with the names of the Roses already printed on them. In order to keep the flowers from unduly expanding on their way to the show, each bloom should be tied round with double Berlin wool. In doing this the outer row of petals should be left free. The best form of tie, as it will not slip and yet can be readily removed, is made by taking one end of a piece of wool about a foot long and twisting it twice round the other end. The loop thus formed is placed over the middle of the bloom and inside the outer or guard petals, and then drawn by the two ends of the tie close round the flower, so as to clasp it firmly and yet not too tightly. Before being left for the night the lid should be put on the box, and the end of a small flower-pot be inserted in the centre of the lid to keep it a few inches open in the front so as to allow of a free access of air to the blooms. For every bloom intended to be staged there should be taken to the show, in a separate box, at least one extra bloom (not necessarily of the same variety), and all these spare blooms should, as a rule, be younger than those in the box designed for the exhibition. It will not be necessary to wire or label these extra blooms, but it will be well to place between the inner petals of each of them a tiny slip of writing paper with the name of the variety upon it, so that there may be no doubt of its identity when selected to take the place of another bloom at the show. The centres of all but the youngest blooms should also be tied. When travelling to the exhibition care must be taken that the Rose boxes are at all times kept level, and for this purpose it will be necessary to personally superintend the placing of the boxes in the vans of the trains, and their removal therefrom, and in the same way to see they are properly treated when travelling by cab or other conveyance.

At the Exhibition.—It is always well to reach the show early, so that plenty of time may be available for setting up the Roses. The boxes intended for exhibition should at once be taken to the places where they are to be staged. In that way their position is secured, and they should not require to be moved after the blooms are once arranged, although this has unfortunately occasionally to be done if the exhibition

EXHIBITION BOX READY FOR THE RECEPTION OF THE BLOOMS.

EXHIBITION BOX WITH BLOOMS ARRANGED.

be in any way crowded. After the lid of the first box to be arranged has been removed, and the box tilted up at the back by means of two small flower-pots, the flowers should in the first instance be untied, and any which are overblown or otherwise unsuitable be taken out of the box and replaced by fresher specimens from the box containing the spare blooms. The largest flowers should be placed in the back row and the smallest in front. As far as practicable the dark and light coloured Roses should be set up alternately so that they may be distributed equally over the box, inserting any yellow flowers there may be towards the centre of the arrangement. It is a good plan to place the two choicest blooms in each row at the ends.

The Roses having been thus arranged as regards colour, the individual flowers should be set up to the required height. Those in the back row should be the highest, those in the front the lowest, and those in the middle row at an intermediate height, but in each row all the blooms should be at the same level. Before finally setting up each bloom it will be necessary to see that it is in exhibition form ; that is to say, in every case any discoloured or ragged petals should be removed, and the outer row of petals firmly but very gradually pressed back at the base into a nearly horizontal position with the help of a large camel's-hair brush. In addition to this the younger blooms may require to have another row or more of petals treated in the same way to help the flower to open ; a sharp puff given with the mouth to the inner petals will also often prove of material assistance in effecting this.

Should any bloom threaten to become too much developed before the judges come round, it will be well to tie up the centre petals again. The flowers having been thus carefully arranged, the lid should be replaced on the box and nearly, but not quite, closed. As soon as the order is given for the box lids to be removed, the lids should be taken off, the few remaining ties removed from the blooms on which they have been replaced, and any final touches to the arrangement given that may be necessary.

Exhibiting Garden or Decorative Roses—Culture and Pruning. — These so-called " garden " Roses belong to such different sections that it is impossible to lay down any special rules as to culture. In all cases, however, the object aimed at should be the same, namely, to obtain strong-growing plants of all the varieties cultivated, to thin out the shoots sparingly, and to prune back lightly those that remain. The climbing varieties should be treated as recommended in the chapter on pruning (p. 300), those of less vigorous growth should be cultivated as free-flowering bushes, while in the case of dwarf-growing Teas and Pompons the same bushy habit should as far as possible be encouraged.

Cutting the Flowers.—As the cutting and arranging of " garden " Roses takes considerably longer than does that of the exhibition varieties, it is advisable to commence operations earlier in the afternoon preceding the show day. In selecting the sprays those on which the most forward flowers are only half open should be chosen, and the remainder should

BARONESS ROTHSCHILD (H.P.)

SOUVENIR DE CATHERINE GUILLOT (*T. Garden Rose*),
COPPERY CARMINE, SHADED ORANGE.

have either well-developed buds or buds just showing colour. Having gathered sufficient shoots of any one sort to make an exhibition bunch, those selected should be wired and placed deeply in a bowl, or other vessel holding plenty of water, before proceeding to cut the remaining bunches. When all are gathered, the sprays should be arranged in bunches and their stems tied together with raffia ready for exhibition on the morrow. Some taste and care are necessary in arranging these bunches so that the flowers are displayed to the best advantage. After this has been done they will require to be again placed in water and removed to a dry cellar or other cool place for the night. On the following morning these bunches must be taken from the receptacles in which they were placed and carefully laid on soft paper in the bottom of a Rose-box from which the tray has been removed, or, better still, in a lady's cardboard dress-box. On arriving at the exhibition the bunches should at once be placed in water in the vases in which they are to be exhibited. The same principle should be followed as when setting up exhibition Roses ; that is to say, the largest bunches should be placed at the back, the smallest in the front, and the light and dark varieties arranged as far as possible alternately, using larger and higher vases for the bunches in the back row than for those in the front. Bunches of garden Roses should not be crowded, or the foliage and habit will not be properly shown.

MRS. JOHN LAING (H.P.), ROSY PINK.

ANNA OLIVIER (T.), PALE BUFF, FLUSHED,

CHAPTER XXII

ROSES UNDER GLASS

To the true lover of the Rose it is a great deprivation to have Roses in flower during less than half the year, which must be the case if they be only cultivated in the open ground. It is, however, possible to have Roses in bloom all the year round if they be grown under glass as well as in the garden, although the supply of blooms may be scanty during the most gloomy part of the winter. For it is the paucity of sunshine and its feeble character which render the growth of the Queen of Flowers under glass in this country so much less satisfactory at that season than in America and other lands where the winter sunshine is stronger and more frequent. To dwellers in the neighbourhood of large towns where Roses cannot be successfully cultivated in the open ground, a Rose house is a great boon, as the plants can there be grown in the soil best suited to their requirements, and the foliage kept clean by frequent syringeing. As roses delight in a free, cool and rather humid atmosphere and in an unrestricted root-run, they do not naturally adapt themselves to ordinary greenhouse culture. If, however, their requirements be understood and complied with as well as the altered circumstances under which they are grown will admit, the cultivation of Roses under glass will not present any difficulties worth mentioning, notwithstanding the fact that the plants will be called upon to flower at a time of year when out-of-doors they would be taking their annual period of rest. There are two ways of growing Roses under glass, each of which has its own distinct advantage : (1) they can be cultivated in pots, or (2) planted out in specially prepared borders.

Roses in Pots.—This is the simplest plan, and the one most frequently adopted, as any light heated greenhouse will answer the purpose. On the other hand, unless certain plants be specially prepared beforehand for late autumn and early winter flowering, others for forcing in heat so as to bloom in the dead of winter, and the remainder to flower from March onwards, the period of blooming is restricted to about a month or six weeks in the spring. The usual custom is for young plants to be purchased in pots from the Rose nurseries in September ready prepared. The plants when received should be placed under a north wall, and allowed to remain there until they are taken into the greenhouse early in December, so as to keep the leaf-buds in a dormant state. Should severe weather set in before this, some protection from frost must be afforded them at night. When housed, ample ventilation should be given, and but little fire heat, or the leaf-buds will begin to push before the plants are pruned at the beginning of January. The pruning of these young plants will be very simple, as the object should mainly be to secure well-developed and strong shoots for another season, rather than to obtain as many flowers as possible the first year. Therefore the weak shoots should be cut clean out, and the remainder shortened back to within two or three eyes. Cool treatment should still be adopted until the young shoots appear, when the heat may be slightly increased, for it should always be borne in mind that the more gradual the progress the plants make, the better will be the ultimate results. For this a steady but moderate warmth should, as far as practicable, be always maintained. Great care must be given to the admission of air, so that the atmosphere in the house may be buoyant and yet without cold draughts. For instance, in ordinary weather the top ventilators should be slightly opened on the side of the house opposite to that from which the wind may at the time be blowing. In very cold or rough weather the ventilators must either be kept closed altogether, or a little air be cautiously admitted in the middle of the day for an hour or so, as circumstances may direct. Another very important point is watering. In the early stages of growth the plants should be kept on rather the dry side, but as the foliage develops the supply of water should be gradually increased. When the flower-buds appear, weak liquid manure may be given at every alternate watering.

Excellent liquid manures may be made by putting half a bushel of either fresh horse droppings or cow manure, or four pounds of soot, into a coarse bag, and

MRS. W. J. GRANT (H.T.), BRIGHT ROSY PINK.

LA FRANCE (H.T.), TWO BLOOMS: SILVERY ROSE WITH PALE LILAC SHADING. ONE BLOOM TO THE LEFT IS SOUVENIR D'ELISE VARDON (T.), CREAM WITH ROSY TINT.

suspending the bag in a tub containing twenty gallons of water. The liquid animal manure may be used for a time, and then as a change the soot water substituted. Much of the success of Rose growing under glass depends upon judicious watering—that is to say, on giving plenty of water whenever the plants really require it, and thus avoiding the objectionable practice of mere surface sprinkling at each time of watering, whatever the requirements of the individual plants at the time may be. Plenty of room should be allowed between the plants, so that light and air can reach all parts of them ; with the same object the best of the new growths when sufficiently long should be secured to light sticks placed near the edge of the pots. At the same time it will be necessary to remove altogether any of the new shoots which may not be required to furnish the plant. Four to six flowering shoots will be found as a rule sufficient for such young plants. At this stage about an inch of the surface soil in the pots should be removed, and a mixture of well-decayed manure and leaf-mould substituted. This surface dressing will tend to keep the roots cool and moist ; it should not, however, be thicker than the soil removed from the pots, or there will not be sufficient space left for watering.

On every fine morning, from the time the Roses are pruned, the plants should be syringed until the new shoots are about an inch in length ; then stop syringeing and sprinkle the floor to keep the atmosphere fairly moist. It may appear strange that in the dull months of the year this " damping down " should be necessary, when the outer atmosphere is mostly so humid, but few people are aware how dry the air in a greenhouse can become under such conditions, and more particularly when there is considerable difference between the inside and outside temperatures. When the plants are in bloom the house should be shaded during the sunniest part of the day, and air admitted to reduce the temperature inside the house. By this means the flowering period will be extended, and the individual flowers will be finer than would otherwise be the case.

Insect and other Pests.—As with such pests in the open ground, so with those in the house, prompt measures are the only safeguard. The three great enemies of the Rose under glass are aphides or greenfly, red spider, and mildew.

Aphides can be readily kept under by fumigation, which should be carried out the evening after the first greenfly is met with, and the dose repeated on the following night. A careful watch should be kept for the reappearance of this pest, and the same plan followed as before. If these directions be only faithfully carried out, greenfly will give little trouble. Richards' X.L. All vaporizing Liquid, or other similar preparation of nicotine, used according to the instructions supplied with it, will be found simple, cleanly, and effectual.

Red Spider.—This usually appears in spring when the air in the house has been allowed to become too dry. In order to destroy this pest the under side of the foliage should be frequently syringed with clear water, and at the same time the plants should not be allowed to become dry at the roots. In addition to this the hot-water pipes should be smeared with sulphur made into a paste by the addition of a little milk.

Mildew.—This is the most troublesome enemy of all to deal with in a Rose house if once allowed to establish itself, but if dealt with very promptly it can readily be kept in check. It most frequently arises from injudicious ventilation causing cold draughts of air to descend upon the tender foliage, for although Roses like a buoyant atmosphere they soon suffer if exposed to a cold current of air, and more particularly if the house has previously been kept too hot or too close. The two great safeguards against mildew are judicious ventilation, and coating the water pipes with sulphur as recommended for red spider as soon as the plants come into leaf. This coating should be renewed about once a fortnight, for nothing will prevent the spores of mildew from finding congenial resting-places more effectually than the fumes of sulphur. However, notwithstanding all these precautions, should the slightest trace of mildew be seen, the plants affected, as well as the plants near them, should be at once dusted over with flowers of sulphur.

Rose Grubs.—In the early stages of growth these should be sought for and destroyed as soon as detected, hand picking being the only effectual remedy. But these pests will not be found nearly as numerous as in the case of Roses grown in the open air.

The Summer Treatment of Pot Plants.—When the plants have flowered more air should gradually be admitted and the temperature gradually lowered so as to prepare them for removal from the house. The middle of June is quite soon enough, as the plants should be encouraged to make new growth before being placed outside. An open spot, handy for watering, should be chosen for the summer quarters of these pot plants, and the pots plunged to their rim in ashes in order to keep the roots cool and to check evaporation. The endeavour at that season should be to obtain strong new growths which will become well ripened by the autumn. For this purpose the wants of the plants should receive frequent attention in the way of watering, the destruction of insect pests, and dusting with sulphur on the first appearance of mildew. All the flower-buds will also require to be removed as they appear. It is to the absence of reasonable care of pot Roses during the summer months that much of the want of success in growing them may often be traced. Occasional waterings with weak liquid manure will be found of much service.

Repotting.—As soon as the plants have flowered, the roots and drainage should be examined. If any plant be found to require moving into a pot a size larger, this must be at once done, taking care to disturb the roots as little as possible, and to ram down the new soil firmly with a potting stick between the pot and the old soil. A suitable compost would be one composed of one half fibrous loam, one quarter old cow manure, and the remaining quarter leaf-mould, sand, and bone meal in equal quantities. Where it is found that the roots have not made

AUGUSTINE GUINOISSEAU (H.T.), WHITE, TINTED BLUSH.

MRS. JOHN LAING, (H.P.), ROSY PINK.

sufficient growth to warrant the plants being repotted, they should be returned to the pots they previously occupied after the drainage has been seen to ; in that case some of the surface soil should be replaced by some of the above-mentioned compost. All the plants may then be well watered. Until the roots have found their way into the new soil and fresh growths have been made, the plants should remain in the greenhouse.

In order to make these instructions as clear and simple as possible, they have been so far confined to the first year's treatment of young plants purchased in the autumn from the nurseries and grown to flower in the following April or May, because, for any one commencing Rose culture under glass, this plan is the easiest and the most satisfactory to follow. There are, however, two other methods which may be afterwards adopted with pot Roses. The plants can be raised from cuttings struck in the way recommended on p. 313, or young plants may be potted up from the open ground, which is far preferable, particularly for H.P.'s and H.T.'s ; in the latter case the plants may either be taken up from the Rose garden, or maiden plants obtained from the Rose nurseries. But whichever plan be adopted, the earlier they can be potted in October, while most of the leaves are still on the plants, the better will be the result.

Having selected a pot of a suitable size, and it should not be larger than will allow reasonable room for the roots, say, from eight to ten inches across, according to the vigour of the plant, all the stronger roots should be shortened, but on the other hand all the fibrous ones retained and without any curtailment. For compost it would be well to use that advised under the head of "Repotting" (p. 360). Do not plant too deeply, as the tendency of the new roots will be to strike downwards, and yet sufficient space must be allowed above for watering. Very firm potting is advisable ; in fact the soil cannot well be made too firm for Roses. When potted the plants should be well watered and then placed under a north wall. After this, until they are taken into the house in December, but little water will be needed. Early in January the plants should be pruned rather hard— that is to say, all the sappy, weak, and crowded shoots should be cut clean out, and the well-ripened ones that remain shortened back to two or three eyes. After this time the plants should be treated throughout the winter, spring, and summer in all respects as has been recommended for young plants purchased in pots from the nurseries (see pp. 353 to 358). The fire heat given should be very moderate, as these Roses have been so recently potted, and therefore but a small proportion of their roots will be as yet in active growth.

Whether the plants are purchased plants, raised from cuttings or potted up from the open ground, they must in the second and following years be submitted to the same routine of treatment as in the first year, except that the pruning should be less severe. A little experience with pot Roses will show that with their roots thus confined the annual growth made is very moderate indeed compared with that of the same varieties in the open ground. Consequently, if pruned as hard, most of the shoots made during the previous summer would be entirely removed ; whereas it is important that as many of these shoots as possible should be retained. After the dead wood and any weak or crowded growths in the centre of the plant have been cut clean out, the remaining shoots of the past season's growth should be pruned from one-third to one-half of their length, according to their strength, the stronger growths being left the longer of the two. The aim should be to obtain a well-balanced plant with a moderate number of good shoots as equally distributed round it as possible. In order to obtain this, it will be advisable after pruning to fasten a wire round the rim of the pot, and to tie out any shoots that may require it to the wire with raffia, taking care not to break any of them in so doing ; or light Hazel sticks may be inserted at intervals round the pots and the shoots secured to them. In the case of very vigorous growers, the leading shoots should be bent spirally round the ring of sticks.

Forcing Roses.—If the plants be required to flower towards the end of the winter instead of in the spring more skill and care will be necessary, for Roses naturally object to much fire heat, and the lack of sunshine at that season is another drawback. For this purpose plants should be selected which have been grown as previously directed for at least one year under glass, with the pots well filled with roots ; or, if preferred, Roses specially prepared for forcing may be purchased. If any repotting be required, it should be done in May. After they have been placed in the house in November very little heat should be at first given, but it may be very gradually increased as the new growths appear. The ventilation should also be gradually lessened. As before recommended, the plants should be frequently syringed until the new growths are about an inch in length ; but after this the floor should, instead, be sprinkled freely with water on all but dull, damp days, or mildew may result. Indeed the great enemy to guard against is mildew, which is a certain sign of some defect in the treatment, either in watering, the admission of air, or the exposure of the plants to sudden changes of temperature.

Roses in Beds.—This is really the most natural way of growing Roses under glass, and if the choice be restricted to the most free-flowering of the Teas and Hybrid Teas, they may, if properly managed, be kept in bloom from the beginning of November till the end of May, or during the entire period that no Roses are obtainable from the open ground, although, as before stated, there may be but very few blooms to be had during January and February.

In order to make this method of growing Roses a complete success, a house should be specially built. A span-roof house running north and south will be best, as the sunshine will then be more equally distributed over it. The walls on the east and west sides should be about three feet high, and the eaves be raised only about a foot above them so as to admit as much light to the plants as possible. The roof should be constructed so that the lights between the main rafters can be entirely removed during the summer months. This is very important, for without some such arrangement the growth of the plants during that season will be arrested by the hot and dry atmosphere within the house, and red spider will with difficulty be kept in check. The beds down each side should be three feet six inches wide so as to allow of two rows of plants; the stronger-growing varieties being placed at the back. If the house be sufficiently wide to allow of a central bed of the same width as the two side beds, this might with advantage be planted with half standards. Ventilators should be inserted in the centre of each light near the ridge so that air may be admitted on either side of the house, as circumstances may direct, and to the extent required.

The spaces allotted for the beds should be cleared out to the depth of two feet eight inches. In the bottom should be placed a layer of stones six inches deep, and above this a layer of gravel or other small stones to the depth of another two inches in order to ensure perfect drainage. The spaces should then be filled up with the compost, consisting of six parts turfy loam rather finely chopped, two parts well-decayed manure, one part leaf mould, and the remaining part half-inch bones and coarse sand in equal quantities. The inner walls supporting the beds need not be more than half a brick thick. The Roses should be planted two feet six inches apart, and in the same way as recommended for outside planting (p. 288). It is advisable to begin with young plants from the open ground, either procured from the Rose nurseries early in November, or taken up in that month from the Rose garden. Any kinds of Roses can be grown in such a Rose house, but Teas are especially recommended on account of their naturally perpetual flowering habit, and also because, more than any other class of Rose, they appreciate the shelter from all adverse weather conditions. Very little warmth should be given, and when young leaves appear at the ends of the shoots these shoots should be cut back half their length. The first winter must necessarily be a barren one, but there may be a moderate number of small blooms in the spring. The same routine of treatment advised for pot Roses under glass should throughout their growth be adopted (see p. 353). In the summer the lights should be entirely removed from the roof, so that the plants, during the hottest part of the year, may be virtually growing in the open air. At the end of that season, if the plants have received due attention as to watering, &c., they should have made good growth. In September the lights should be replaced on the roof, but ample ventilation should be given, and water entirely withheld, in order to give the plants as far as possible a period of rest. In October they will require pruning—that is to say, some of the weak and crowded shoots should be removed, and the remainder shortened back about one-third of their length. After a week the plants should be well watered with clear water and syringed every morning, the floor of the house at the same time being freely wetted. Should the nights a little later prove cold, some fire heat should be given, but only enough to keep the plants slowly growing. On all bright days the top ventilators may be opened on the side opposite to that quarter from which the wind happens to be blowing. On the appearance of the flower-buds, very weak liquid manure should be given liberally once a fortnight.

As the weather becomes colder more heat will have to be given, but the temperature should not be allowed to rise above sixty degrees in the day-time or to fall lower than forty-five degrees at night. In this way a fair number of flowers may be obtained until about Christmas, and a flower here and there until March. If the plants be again lightly pruned in January, with the help of increasing sunshine there will be a goodly number until nearly June. The lights must once more be taken from the roof and the same routine as before followed in preparation for the third year's crop of flowers, in the late autumn, winter and spring.

Climbing Roses under Glass.—Nothing has been before said about climbing Roses. They are un-suitable for any house specially devoted to Roses, because they shut out so much of that sunlight from the other Roses which is so needful for their welfare throughout the winter and early spring months.

These rampant varieties should therefore be grown in other houses where their presence will be less objectionable. Climbing Roses, whether dwarf plants or on standards, are best planted outside the greenhouse in a well-cultivated and manured border and their leading shoots brought into it and trained up the roof. They should be pruned after they have flowered, and each year a good deal of the older wood removed in order to make room for the shoots which will be formed during the current year, and thus enable them to become well ripened before the winter sets in. As a protection against injury from frost, hay-bands may with advantage be wound round the stocks of the standards outside the house early in December, and some bracken or other dry and light material placed over the exposed portion of the dwarf plants.

TEA ROSE SOUVENIR D'ELISE VARDON.

CHAPTER XXIII

SOME LISTS OF THE BEST ROSES FOR VARIOUS USES

ABBREVIATIONS, &C., USED IN THE FOLLOWING LISTS

A. Autumn-flowering. Roses which flower in the summer, and again, with more or less freedom, in the autumn.

S. Summer-flowering. Roses which only flower once within a year.

Cl. Poly. Climbing Polyantha.

H.C. Hybrid China.
H.N. Hybrid Noisette.
H.P. Hybrid Perpetual.
H.T. Hybrid Tea.
N. Noisette.
Pom. Pompon.
Sin. Single-flowered.

BY "exhibition Roses" is meant those varieties which are sufficiently large and perfect in form to be staged as separate blooms in boxes at the exhibitions.

By "garden Roses" is meant all other varieties which are never so exhibited—except in those cases where an exhibition Rose is described as good both for exhibition and for garden decoration.

SELECT LIST OF ROSES FOR EXHIBITION

In the following selections the varieties have been arranged, under their different colours, according to the average number of times they were staged in the prize stands at the recent leading exhibitions of the National Rose Society.

EXHIBITION ROSES

HYBRID PERPETUALS AND HYBRID TEAS

WHITE AND CREAM

Bessie Brown (H.T.).
Kaiserin Augusta Victoria (H.T.).

Marchioness of Londonderry.
Margaret Dickson.
White Lady (H.T.).

N.B.—Mildred Grant (H.T.); a lovely new creamy white variety; it should be included in every exhibitor's collection, however small.

PINK AND PALE ROSE

Mrs. John Laing.
Caroline Testout (H.T.).
Mrs. W. J. Grant (H.T.).
Her Majesty.
Mrs. R. G. Sharman-Craw-
ford.

La France (H.T.).
Madame Gabriel Luizet.
Ulster.
Killarney (H.T.).
Baroness Rothschild.

MEDIUM RED AND ROSE

Ulrich Brunner.
Marquise Litta (H.T.)
Gustave Piganeau.
Suzanne M. Rodocanachi.
François Michelon.

Helen Keller.
Dupuy Jamain.
Etienne Levet.
Tom Wood.
Duchesse de Morny.

CRIMSON

A. K. Williams.
Captain Hayward.
Alfred Colomb.
Marie Baumann.
Fisher Holmes.
Victor Hugo.

Comte de Raimbaud.
General Jacqueminot.
Duke of Edinburgh.
Dr. Andry.
E. Y. Teas.
Duchess of Bedford.

N.B.—The latest addition in this colour is Ben Cant, a most promising new Hybrid Perpetual.

DARK CRIMSON

Horace Vernet.
Earl of Dufferin.
Prince Arthur.
Charles Lefèbvre.

Duke of Wellington.
Louis Van Houtte.
Xavier Olibo.

TEAS AND NOISETTES
WHITE AND CREAM

White Maman Cochet.
The Bride.
Innocente Pirola.
Souvenir de S. A. Prince.

Muriel Grahame.
Souvenir d'Élise Vardon.
Niphetos.

PINK AND PALE ROSE

Maman Cochet.
Catherine Mermet.
Madame Cusin.
Bridesmaid.
Mrs. Edward Mawley.

Souvenir d'un Ami.
Madame de Watteville.
Ernest Metz.
Cleopatra.

YELLOW, BUFF, AND ORANGE

Comtesse de Nadaillac.
Madame Hoste.
Maréchal Niel (N.).
Medea.

Marie Van Houtte.
Caroline Kuster (N.).
Anna Olivier.

N.B.—Lady Roberts, a beautiful salmon pink sport from Anna Olivier, judging by the blooms recently exhibited, promises to be a charming addition to the Tea and Noisette section.

GARDEN OR DECORATIVE ROSES

In the following list the varieties have been arranged according to the number of times they were staged in the prize stands at the Exhibition held last year in the

Temple Gardens, which was an unusually large and representative one :—

Gustave Régis (H.T.).
Marquise de Salisbury (H.T.).
William Allen Richardson (N.)
Madame Pernet Ducher (H.T.).
Rosa macrantha (Sin.).
Turner's Crimson Rambler (Cl. Poly.).
Camoëns (H.T.).
Madame Chédane Guinoisseau (T.).
Bardou Job (H.T.).
Alister Stella Gray (N.).
L'Idéal (N.).
Madame Falcot (T.).
Reine Olga de Wurtemberg (H.T.).
Souvenir de Catherine Guillot (T.).
Paul's Carmine Pillar (Sin.).

The Garland (H.C.).
Claire Jacquier (Cl. Poly.).
Anne of Geierstein (Sweet-brier).
Laurette Messimy (C.).
Ma Capucine (T.).
Mignonette (Pom.).
Papillon (T.).
Paul's Single White (Sin.).
Crested Moss (Moss).
Homère (T.).
Perle d'Or (Pom.).
Rosa moschata alba (Sin.).
Rosa Mundi (Damask).
Brenda (Sweet-brier).
Madame Pierre Cochet (T.).
Meg Merrilies (Sweet-brier).
Red Damask (Damask).
Rosa himalayaca (Sin.).
Rosa lucida plena.

THE BEST ROSES FOR GROWING UNDER GLASS

Anna Olivier (T.).
Baroness Rothschild (H.P.)
Bridesmaid (T.).
Captain Hayward (H.P.).
Catherine Mermet (T.).
Caroline Testout (H.T.).
General Jacqueminot (H.P.).
Innocente Pirola (T.).
La France (H.T.).
Liberty (H.T.).
Madame de Watteville (T.).
Madame Hoste (T.).
Madame Lambard (T.).
Marie Van Houtte (T.).
Merveille de Lyon (H.P.).

Mrs. John Laing (H.P.).
Mrs. R. G. Sharman - Crawford (H.P.).
Mrs. W. J. Grant (H.T.).
Niphetos (T.).
Perle des Jardins (T.).
Souvenir de S. A. Prince (T.).
Souvenir d'un Ami (T.).
S. M. Rodocanachi (H.P.).
Sunrise (T.).
The Bride (T.).
Ulrich Brunner (H.P.).
Viscountess Folkestone (H.T.)

CLIMBING VARIETIES

Climbing Niphetos (T.).

Climbing Perle des Jardins (T.).

Fortune's Yellow (N.).

Maréchal Niel (N.).

Turner's Crimson Rambler (Cl. Poly.).

William Allen Richardson(N.).

In the following list will be found, alphabetically arranged, a selection from the choicest varieties of Roses now in cultivation. The varieties marked with an asterisk make good standards :—

Aimée Vibert (N.).—Pure white ; late flowering ; very vigorous and almost evergreen. Flowers in clusters. (A.)

A. K. Williams (H.P.).—Carmine ; early flowering and of moderate growth. One of the most perfect in form of all exhibition Roses. (A.)

* *Alfred Colomb* (H.P.).—Carmine ; late flowering ; vigorous, and fragrant. A fine exhibition variety. (A.)

Alister Stella Gray (N.).—Pale yellow ; a good climbing Rose ; flowers in clusters. Flowers again in the autumn. (A.)

Anna Olivier (T.).—Pale buff ; vigorous ; charming under glass, but the flowers in the open ground are easily damaged by wet. (A.)

Antoine Rivoire (H.T.).—Vigorous ; a good cream-coloured garden Rose. (A.)

Augustine Guinoisseau (H.T.).—Blush white ; vigorous ; very free flowering, known as the " White La France," but the flowers are neither as large nor as full as La France. (A.)

Austrian Copper (Austrian Brier).—Coppery red inside of petal, and old gold outside ; vigorous. The most beautiful of all single-flowered Roses. (S.)

Austrian Yellow (Austrian Brier).—Yellow ; vigorous. Like the foregoing, except as regards colour. (S.)

Bardou Job (H.T).—Crimson ; vigorous ; bears large beautifully shaded flowers which are almost single. (A.)

Baroness Rothschild (H.P.).—Pink; upright growth; late flowering and good in colour. Scentless. (A.)

Beauté Inconstante (N.).—Metallic red shaded yellow; vigorous. Distinct and charming in colour, but variable in this respect, as its name implies. (A.)

Beauty of Waltham (H.P.).—Crimson. A useful exhibition Rose. (A.)

Ben Cant (H.P.).—Crimson; vigorous. A new and welcome addition to the crimson exhibition Roses. (A.)

Bennett's Seedling, or *Thoresbyana* (Ayrshire).—White; one of the very best and hardiest summer-flowering climbing Roses. Blooms in clusters. (S.)

Bessie Brown (H.T.).—Creamy white; vigorous. Although only sent out in 1899 it was last year to be seen in nearly every exhibition stand. The first of the really good whites among the H.P.'s and H.T.'s. (A.)

Bouquet d'Or (T.).—Dark yellow; very vigorous. The best of the Gloire de Dijon race in flower and habit of growth; but not so free-flowering as Gloire de Dijon. Fragrant. (A.)

Bridesmaid (T.).—Pink; moderately vigorous. A deep-coloured sport from Catherine Mermet, one of the best exhibition Teas. (A.)

Camoëns (H.T.).—Rose; vigorous. A pretty free-flowering garden Rose. (A.)

Captain Hayward (H.P.).—Crimson; vigorous. One of the best crimson Roses for exhibition; not very full, but has fine petals of great substance. (A.)

Caroline Testout (H.T.).—Pink; vigorous. Takes a high position both as an exhibition and garden Rose. Fragrant. (A.)

Catherine Mermet (T.).—Pale pink; moderately vigorous. One of the best exhibition Teas, and, like nearly all the sports from it, has the most perfectly formed flowers of all the Teas. (A.)

Cecile Brunner (Pom.).—Pink; dwarf. The best of the pink Pompons. (A.)

Charles Lefèbvre (H.P.).—Dark crimson; vigorous. An old exhibition Rose, which has never been equalled in its particular form and colour; few Roses are as beautiful when it is at its best. Fragrant. (A.)

Claire Jacquier (Cl. Poly.).—Nankeen yellow; a remarkably vigorous summer-flowering climber. Flowers in clusters. Not quite hardy. (S.)

Clara Watson (H.T).—Rosy cream; vigorous. A free-flowering garden Rose. (A.)

Common or *Old Moss* (Moss).—Pink; vigorous; one of the oldest Roses grown, but still the best of all the Mosses. Fragrant. (S.)

Common Provence or *Cabbage Rose* (Provence). — Pink; moderately vigorous; also one of our oldest Roses, but still unequalled in its class. (S.)

Common Sweet-brier (Sweet-brier). — Pale pink; vigorous, foliage deliciously fragrant. (S.)

Common Monthly or *Old Blush* (China).—Pink; vigorous. The most perpetual flowering of all Roses. (A.)

Comte de Raimbaud (H.P.).—Crimson; vigorous, a fine crimson Rose for exhibition. (A.)

Comtesse de Nadaillac (T.).—Peach shaded apricot; growth moderate; grand exhibition Tea Rose. When at its best no Tea Rose is as beautiful. Not an easy Rose to grow. (A.)

Cramoisi Supérieur (China).—Crimson; moderately vigorous. The best of the crimson Chinas. (A.)

Dr. Andry (H.P.).—Crimson; vigorous; a strong-growing exhibition and garden Rose. (A.)

Dr. Grill (T.).—Pale rosy fawn; moderately vigorous. A distinct and free-flowering garden Rose. (A.)

Duke of Edinburgh (H.P.).—Scarlet crimson; vigorous. A bright and strong-growing exhibition and garden Rose. (A.)

Félicité-Perpétue (Evergreen).—Creamy white. One of the best white summer-flowering climbing Roses. Blooms in clusters of rosette-shaped flowers. (S.)

Fellenberg (China).—Crimson ; vigorous ; a good crimson in this free-flowering section. (A.)

*_Fisher Holmes_ (H.P.).—Crimson ; vigorous. A good exhibition and garden Rose. (A.)

*_General Jacqueminot_ (H.P.).—Crimson ; vigorous ; one of the oldest of the H.P.'s. An excellent exhibition and garden Rose. Fragrant. (A.)

*_Gloire de Dijon_ (T.).—Buff. The most free-flowering of all climbing Roses, and for general usefulness has no equal. Fragrant. (A.)

Gloire Lyonnaise (H.T.).—Lemon white ; vigorous upright habit. A good and distinct garden Rose. (A.)

Gloire des Polyantha (Pom.).—Rose ; dwarf ; an excellent rose-coloured Pompon. (A.)

G. Nabonnand (T.).—Pale flesh ; vigorous ; one of the best garden Roses of its colour. (A.)

Grüss an Teplitz (H.T.).—Crimson ; vigorous. Unequalled as a free-flowering crimson garden Rose ; a fine acquisition. (A.)

Gustave Piganeau (H.P.).—Shaded carmine; growth moderate ; a fine and trustworthy exhibition Rose ; but by no means an easy Rose to grow in many soils. (A.)

Gustave Regis (H.T.).—Nankeen yellow ; vigorous. The best and most vigorous of the yellow garden Roses. (A.)

Harrisonii (Austrian Brier).—Yellow ; vigorous. A very pretty summer-flowering garden Rose. (S.)

Her Majesty (H.P.).—Pale rose ; vigorous upright habit. Flowers very large. A very fine late-flowering exhibition Rose. It is very subject to mildew and is scentless. (A.)

Horace Vernet (H.P.).—Dark crimson ; growth moderate. The most beautiful dark exhibition Rose in cultivation. By no means an easy Rose to grow in many localities.

In some gardens it grows as vigorously as other H.P.'s, but in most places it makes but very poor growth. (A.)

Innocente Pirola (T.).—Creamy white. A fine exhibition Tea, rather subject to mildew. (A.)

Janet's Pride (Sweet-brier).—White, tipped crimson ; vigorous. Almost single-flowered. One of the best of the hybrid Sweet-briers. (S.)

*Kaiserin Augusta Victoria (H.T.).—Cream; vigorous. One of the best of the white, or nearly white, exhibition H.T.'s. There is a climbing variety of this Rose which promises to be a great acquisition. (A.)

Killarney (H.T.).—Pale pink ; vigorous ; already a great favourite. A good Rose for exhibition, and still more valuable for garden decoration. (A.)

Lady Penzance (Sweet-brier).—Coppery yellow. The most charming of all the hybrid Sweet-briers. It is said to be a cross between the common Sweet-brier and Austrian Copper. (S.)

*La France (H.T.).—Pale rose; vigorous. A hardy and very free-flowering exhibition and garden Rose. Fragrant. (A.)

*Laurette Messimy (China).—Rose ; vigorous. A lovely semi-double continuous-flowering garden Rose. (A.)

L'Idéal (N.).—Metallic red ; vigorous. A strong-growing garden Rose. Distinct and charming in colour. (A.)

Longworth Rambler (H.T.).—Crimson. The best of all the red climbing Roses on account of its freedom of flowering in the autumn. (A.)

Ma Capucine (T.).—Bronzy yellow, shaded red ; of moderate growth. The best of all the button-hole Roses ; quite distinct in colour. (A.)

Madame Abel Chatenay (H.T.).—Salmon pink ; vigorous. The best garden Rose in its colour. (A.)

Madame Alfred Carrière (H.N.).—White. The best white climbing Rose. (A.)

Madame Anna Marie de Montravel (Pom.).—Dwarf. The best of the white Pompons. (A.)

Madame Chédane Guinoisseau (T.). — Yellow; moderately vigorous. A fine button-hole Rose. (A.)

Madame Cusin (T.).—Pale rose; upright growth. A good exhibition Tea; rather tender. (A.)

Madame de Watteville (T.).—Cream-edged rose; vigorous. A very distinct and pretty exhibition Tea; rather tender. (A.)

Madame Eugène Resal (China).—Coppery rose; vigorous. Much like Laurette Messimy, but deeper in colour. (A.)

Madame Gabriel Luizet (H.P.).—Pink; vigorous. An excellent early-flowering exhibition Rose. It seldom flowers in the autumn. (S.)

Madame Hoste (T.).—Lemon yellow; vigorous. A fine exhibition and garden Rose. (A.)

Madame Jules Grolez (H.T.).—Clear rose; vigorous. A very distinct and free-flowering garden Rose. (A.)

Madame Lambard (T.).—Salmon shaded rose; vigorous. A good and continuous-flowering garden Tea. Very variable in colour. (A.)

*Maman Cochet (T.).—Pale pink; vigorous. A fine addition to the exhibition and garden Teas. (A.)

Marchioness of Londonderry (H.P.).—Ivory white; vigorous erect growth. Large petals of great substance. A good exhibition Rose. Colour too often a very unpleasant shade of white. (A.)

Maréchal Niel (N.).—Golden yellow; very vigorous. The finest yellow Rose in cultivation. Fragrant. Very subject to canker. (A.)

Marie Baumann (H.P.).—Soft carmine-red; moderately vigorous. A good exhibition Rose. Fragrant. (A.)

*Marie Van Houtte (T.).—Lemon yellow edged rose; vigorous. A charming exhibition and garden Tea of good growth. (A.)

*Marquise Litta (H.T.).—Carmine rose; vigorous. A fine and distinct early-flowering exhibition and garden Rose. (A.)

Meg Merrilies (Sweet-brier).—Crimson; very vigorous. One of the best of the Penzance Sweet-briers. (S.)

Mildred Grant (H.T.).—White; vigorous. This variety promises to be one of the most beautiful white Roses in the Hybrid Tea section ever raised, and consequently will be a great acquisition to the exhibitor. (A.)

Mrs. Bosanquet (China).—Pale flesh; vigorous; very free-flowering. (A.)

Mrs. Edward Mawley (T.).—Pink, tinted carmine; moderately vigorous; very free-flowering. Although only sent out in 1899 it has already taken a high position among the exhibition Teas. (A.)

*Mrs. *John Laing* (H.P.).—Rosy pink; vigorous. Few Roses have so many good qualities. It is hardy, of good growth, and free-flowering, and almost as good in the garden as in the show. (A.)

*Mrs. *R. G. Sharman-Crawford* (H.P.).—Rosy pink. Beautiful in colour, and a fine early-flowering exhibition and garden Rose. (A.)

Mrs. W. J. Grant (H.T.).—Rosy pink; moderately vigorous; distinct in form and colour, and one of the best of our exhibition Roses. There is a climbing variety of this Rose which promises to be a great acquisition to the dwarf climbers. (A.)

Muriel Grahame (T.).—Pale cream; moderately vigorous. Has all the good qualities as an exhibition Tea of the fine variety, Catherine Mermet, from which it sported. (A.)

Paul's Carmine Pillar (Sin.).—Carmine; very vigorous. The most beautiful red, climbing, single-flowered Rose that has yet been raised. (S.)

Perle des Rouges (Pom.).—Crimson; dwarf. The best of the red Pompons. (A.)

Persian Yellow (Austrian Brier).—Golden yellow; vigorous. There is no other Rose in cultivation of the same bright shade of yellow. It does not succeed in all localities, and is the first Rose to feel the effects of a smoke-laden atmosphere. (S.)

*Prince Arthur (H.P.).—Shaded crimson; vigorous. A good exhibition and garden Rose. (A.)

Prince Camille de Rohan (H.P.).—Crimson maroon; vigorous. The best dark crimson Rose for garden decoration. (A.)

Reine Marie Henriette (H.T.).—Cherry carmine. A valuable red climbing Rose on account of its autumn-flowering qualities. (A.)

Reine Olga de Wurtemberg (H.T.).—Crimson. Almost a summer-flowering climbing Rose, as it yields so few blooms in the autumn. There is no red climber to equal it in colour. (S.)

Rêve d'Or (N.).—Buff yellow. A very vigorous, free-flowering climber. Not quite hardy. (A.)

Rosa alpina (Sin.).—Rose; vigorous. Interesting on account of its being thornless, and also as the earliest of all Roses to bloom. (S.)

Rosa macrantha (Sin.).—Flesh. One of the best of the single-flowered climbers. Rather subject to mildew. (S.)

Rosa moschata = Brunoni (Sin.).—White; a vigorous climbing Rose, producing clusters of small white flowers. (S.)

Rosa multiflora (Sin.), also known as *Rosa polyantha simplex* (single-flowered).—White; a vigorous climber, producing large bunches of tiny white flowers. *Rosa multiflora grandiflora* is of similar growth, but the individual flowers are much larger. (S.)

Rosa Mundi (Gallica).—Red, striped white; moderately vigorous. The best of the so-called York and Lancaster Roses. (S.)

Rosa rubrifolia (Sin.).—Rose; very vigorous. The flowers are insignificant, but the foliage is quite distinct from that of all other Roses, being of a peculiar purplish-red shade. (S.)

Rosa sinica Anemone (single-flowered).—Pink shaded Rose; vigorous. Both the large single flowers and delicate glossy foliage are alike beautiful. (S.)

Souvenir d'Élise Vardon (T.).—Cream ; growth moderate. A fine exhibition Tea, but a difficult Rose to cultivate on account of its weak growth. (A.)

Souvenir de Catherine Guillot (T.).—Growth moderate. A distinct and charming button-hole Rose. A vigorous-growing Rose of the same unique colour would be a great acquisition. (A.)

Souvenir de la Malmaison (Bourbon).—Blush white ; vigorous. One of the oldest Roses grown. A hardy and free-flowering garden Rose. (A.)

Souvenir de S. A. Prince (T.).—White ; vigorous. A good white exhibition and garden Tea. (A.)

Souvenir du President Carnot (H.T.).—White ; vigorous. A very free-flowering garden Rose. (A.)

Stanwell Perpetual (Scotch).—Pale blush. One of the earliest and latest garden Roses to flower. Fragrant. (A.)

*Suzanne M. Rodocanachi (H.P.).—Glowing rose ; vigorous. A lovely exhibition and garden Rose. (A.)

The Bride (T.).—White ; moderately vigorous. Has all the good qualities as an exhibition Rose of the fine variety, Catherine Mermet, from which it sported. (A.)

The Garland (H.C.).—Blush. A very old summer-flowering climber of distinct habit and foliage. (S.)

Turner's Crimson Rambler (Cl. Poly.).—Crimson. A remarkably vigorous climber ; flowers freely in clusters. Few climbing Roses in recent years have been so largely grown. (S.)

* Ulrich Brunner (H.P.).—Cherry red. One of the most vigorous of all the H.P.'s. Fine both as an exhibition and garden Rose. (A.)

Victor Hugo (H.P.).—Bright crimson ; moderately vigorous. The brightest crimson of all the exhibition H.P.'s. (A.)

* Viscountess Folkestone (H.T.).—Creamy white ; vigorous ; free-flowering. The most charming white, or nearly white, garden Rose. (A.)

White Banksian and *Yellow Banksian.*—Both are very old climbing Roses, bearing clusters of small double flowers. Being tender they will only thrive out-of-doors in warm and sheltered situations. (S.)

* *White Maman Cochet* (T.).—White; vigorous. The best exhibition and garden Tea Rose of recent introduction. (A.)

White Pet (China).—White; vigorous. May be best described as a dwarf-growing and free-flowering *Félicité-Perpétue.* (A.)

Wichuriana (Sin.).—White; very vigorous. A new type of Rose which has a trailing habit, and late in the summer bears a large number of small white flowers. The foliage is small and shining. (S.)

* *William Allen Richardson* (N.).—Deep orange, with white edges. A most distinct and valuable climbing Rose. Early in the season the flowers often come almost white. (A.)

A good many charming Roses are unavoidably omitted from the above list, but sufficient have been mentioned to show the wealth of really good varieties for all purposes now available.

INDEX

The Antique Collectors' Club

The Antique Collectors' Club has 12,000 members and the monthly journal (not August), sent free to members, discusses in more depth than is normal for a collectors' magazine the type of antiques and art available to collectors. It is the only British antiques magazine which has consistently grown in circulation over the past decade.

The Antique Collectors' Club also publishes a series of books on antique furniture, art reference and horology, together with various standard works connected with arts and antiques. It also publishes a series of practical books, invaluable to collectors, under the general heading of the Price Guide Series (price revision lists published annually).

New titles are being added to the list at the rate of about ten a year. Why not ask for an updated catalogue?

The Antique Collectors' Club
5 Church Street, Woodbridge, Suffolk, England
Telephone 03943 5501

Other books by Gertrude Jekyll published by the Antique Collectors' Club

Colour Schemes for the Flower Garden
8½ ins. × 5½ ins./22cm × 14cm. 328 pages, 120 black and white illustrations, 32 in colour. Generally thought to be the author's best book. Her sense of colour, thoughts on 'painting' a garden and imaginative ideas on planting arrangements make this book a joy to read.

Home and Garden
8½ ins. × 5½ ins./22cm × 14cm. 373 pages. 53 black and white illustrations, 16 in colour. In this book Gertrude Jekyll introduces us to her life both as gardener and craftswoman, and discusses in detail the building of her home — Munstead Wood designed by Edwin Lutyens.

Wood and Garden
8½ ins. × 5½ ins./22cm × 14cm. 380 pages, 71 black and white illustrations, 32 in colour. The first book Jekyll wrote takes the reader through her gardening year month by month. Also included are her practical and critical thoughts on the herbaceous garden, woodland, large and small gardens, and other gardening topics.

For full list write to:
Antique Collectors' Club, Church Street, Woodbridge, Suffolk, England

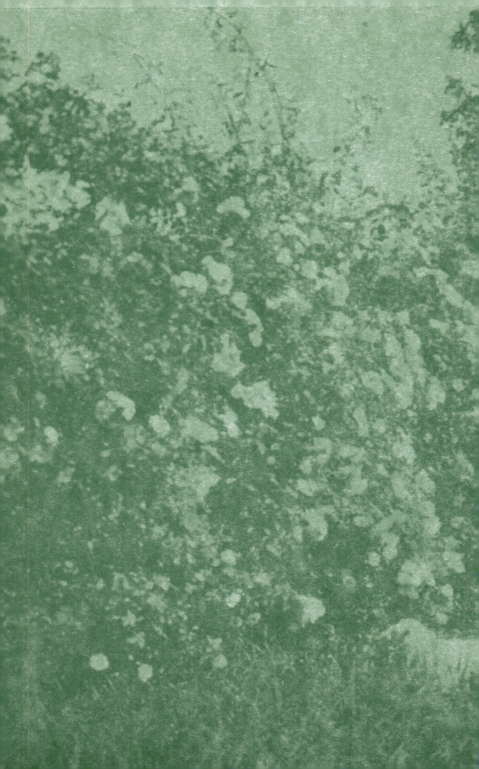